Mom Died Last Night

My shared death experience

A memoir of death, grief, and afterlife communication

Mom Died Last Night

My shared death experience

A memoir of death, grief, and afterlife communication

By Liz Peterson

Raise The Vibe Books

First Printing: 2023

eBook- ISBN: 979-8-9870619-0-9

Paperback- ISBN: 979-8-9870619-1-6

Library of Congress Control Number: 2022922432

Comments and inquiries regarding this book may be sent to the author at www.lizshealingtouch.com

For updates and information, please follow @raisethevibewithliz on social media

Published by Liz Peterson /

Raise The Vibe Books, LLC.

Vashon, WA 98070

Editing: Elke Macartney

Book layout and design: Liz Peterson

Cover art/design: Liz Peterson and FIVVER, sam_4321

Book Cover design: FIVVER, sam_4321

Back Cover Photo: Rick Dahms

This book is dedicated to my mother,

May she rest in peace and know that

I will love her always

Foreword

Before mom passed away, we both had dreams where I was pregnant with twins. She called one morning and said she had a dream I was pregnant with twins and I had the same dream a few days earlier.

In dream interpretation, being pregnant in a dream can mean you are pregnant with an idea or creation, or about to birth something new into the world. A month before her death, on the super full moon in January, I dreamt I walked into a women's birthing center. A woman takes me to get a sonogram, and I look down at my tag and see there are two names on it. I realize I'm having twins, and I ask, "Are all the babies going to be born tonight?"

After her death I continued to have dreams about pregnancy: 4 months after, I'm still pregnant, but wondering if I'm caring for the pregnancy like I should have been. A few months after that, I dreamt about an infant in my arms, which to me meant I had birthed my idea into existence: I believe it is this book. And in yet another dream, I had older twins.

Now it's late October, I'm on a flight to Oahu and I remember a dream I'd had this morning. Once again I dreamt about a child and heard the child asking to be fed. It was time to nurture the "baby"—which is very much the stage I'm in before publishing this book: I'm nurturing and feeding this baby with what it takes for the child to thrive: editing, cover design, code assignment, planning the launch....

It dawns on me that my mother has been a part of this process from the beginning. While she was alive, with her precognitive dream of my pregnancy with twins, she unknowingly knew I was going to be birthing something new into reality. And in her afterlife, she still communicated with me. She pressed upon me to write. She let me know she was still with me. And she maintained our connection across the veil.

She has been with me every step of the way to publishing. From before death when she shared her dream with me, and now from beyond, I know without a doubt our communication will continue.

By the way, you might be wondering, and I have too: Why did mom and I have dreams about twins? I feel that the second twin is the new career path I'll be on as I birth this book. Thank you mom for confirming my new path. I'll walk it with pride, and in your honor.

Chapter 1
The night mom died

I had just arrived home from the hospital when I got a call from my sister Connie just before 10:OO PM. She'd heard from the doctor, who told her that they'd done all they could, mom wasn't responding, and she may not make it through the night. The doctor had asked if we wanted a DNR—do-not-resuscitate—order. None of which I expected to hear. I paused, then began to cry. Tearfully, we decided that even though we selfishly wanted her to stay, she wouldn't be happy staying in her body if it couldn't give her the freedom she desired. We cried together for a few minutes, then said goodbye so she could call our younger sister Sara.

Thirty minutes later she called back. The hospital had called again, "They said mom's organs are shutting down, there's nothing more they can do. They said that we have permission to go to the hospital and say goodbye." Connie said that Sara had already left her home for the hospital, and my oldest niece Brita was driving her, even though Brita would not be able to enter the hospital. I checked the ferry schedule—the next boat was at 10:55 PM. I live on an island in the middle of Puget Sound, and this was the only way off. I could make the last boat off the south end of the island. I hung up and ran for the ferry.

Connie checked back in, and filled me in on what we'd been instructed do when we reached the hospital. "Go to the E.R. entrance when you get there. They'll check you in and escort you to the ICU." I said, "I'll talk to you when I arrive," and we said goodbye. I decided to call an old friend I'd recently reconnected with from Maryland to keep me company and for support as I made the drive to the hospital—45 minutes away. I felt as if I may not make it to the hospital in time, which seemed like a lifetime away. But I'm glad I had someone to talk to and I wasn't alone.

When I arrived, I headed into the emergency room entrance. I had to go through a health check just inside the entry door. "Hello again. I'd been here earlier today." The staff member had me change my mask, use hand sanitizer, then wrote my name and the time on her clipboard, and pointed me to the guard at the front desk for the next step. I walked up to the security guard. He asked my name, and for a drivers license, and proof of a negative covid test. I showed him a picture on my phone of the test I'd done earlier that morning, and he questioned me, "When did you do it?" Me: "I was here earlier, I don't have the original, I threw it away when I left and didn't think I'd be back tonight. Here's a picture of it. I held it in front of my car clock/radio this morning." I thought, thank goodness I followed my intuition and took a picture of it. "Let me see it again." He says. "What's the date?" I thought, "Really? You know why I'm here. You're taking too long; my mother is going to die before I get up there!" I noticed my impatience start to show as I sighed and looked to the left of me. Mind you, it was almost midnight. He input the info, went to print the sticker I'm to wear.... Oh wait, now he needed to change the color of the sticker tape because It's almost the next day... but it's not. "Does it really matter? Really? Right now?" I thought to myself as he fumbled with the machine. I grew more impatient and worried that I was not going to make it upstairs before my mother passes away. He finally got it printed— it's 11:56 PM. He handed me the sticker I'm supposed to wear and said, "Follow me". We slowly walk through the emergency room to the elevator outside the hall and silently ride up to the ICU on the 4th floor. He walked me in through the sliding security doors where he passed me off to a floor nurse who awkwardly ushered me past the nurse's station, a few rooms, and partly down the hall. She had an interesting "Should I say something?" look on her face and stumbled around her words as she directed me to mom's room.

I entered mom's room knowing something was off.

"She just passed!" my younger sister Sara said. She was crying and talking to my older sister on the phone. She'd made it to her bedside thirty minutes prior to me, and was able to say goodbye before mom's heart stopped. She began to share that she'd read letters to mom that her kids had written to her. While she was reading the letters, she looked at mom and a tear had come out of her eye, rolling down mom's temple. She'd told mom her

goodbyes and held the phone to mom's ear so my older sister Connie could say goodbye to her too.

On one hand, I felt grateful that Sara had made it to the hospital in time. And I felt as though Mom waited to die until after she had arrived and said her goodbyes. But I have to admit, it stung a bit: the disappointment that I'd not made it in time to say a final goodbye before her last breath. To not be there when she transitioned. Not have that last experience with her. But I knew it was a good thing that Sara had that time with mom alone to say her goodbyes. They'd both needed it, and whether mom was conscious or not, it was important.

I said my goodbyes to mom just six hours earlier that evening. I'd spent the afternoon by her side holding her hand, talking with her, pleading with her to keep fighting and come back to us. I watched the nurses come in and out of her room, sharing what was happening as things beeped and called for their attention throughout the day. With all the things it seemed they had to do to keep mom's vitals regulated, something told me that it may have been time to say my goodbyes. I had a feeling she may not have long, but I was afraid to lose hope. When it came time for me to leave, I didn't know whether to stay or to go. I went back and forth in my mind, trying to make a decision before settling on leaving the hospital around dinner time to eat and head home.

This was a decision I'd later regret.

After speaking to the attending doctor on the way out, I even went back into the room to say a second goodbye. With my hand on her soft hair, I told her I loved her and kissed her on her forehead. I knew somehow then. It was the look on the doctor's face as he talked to me, telling me about the different things they were trying, and asking if it was okay to administer something through her IV after I left. He had a look of worry and compassion, a slight furrow in his brow, a "should I say something?" look. And even though I didn't want to think it, and prayed for a different outcome, I had an uneasy feeling that she was going to pass on. I suppose the whole time I felt as though she was passing. That the Reiki I'd given her may help her to pass instead of help her heal. I just didn't want to own that this outcome could be true or believe she'd choose to go. I'd hoped for longer with her. That she'd surprise us and get lucid. Maybe even have a rush of aliveness before she passed so I could talk to her one last time. All were false hopes and desires to avoid feeling the inevitable loss of my mother. Denial. In my mind I would head home, and Sara would be by her side tomorrow, and Connie would see her when she got back the following day, Sunday. I had shared that with the doctor in our conversation. Maybe that look on his face was reflecting the thought, "This poor woman does not want to see the reality that her mother is dying."

———

I looked from my sister to my lifeless mother lying there on the bed—up and down the length of her, and to either side of her where the equipment that had kept tabs on her condition earlier. She was the same as I'd left her, but a silence had set in. She was pale. No movement. No machines animated her. No more hospital sounds. I moved closer to the side of the bed and placed my hands first on the bedrail, then on her hand. We both stood by, gazing at her. After hugging my sister, I took a seat next to mom. I proceeded to call my 4 boys, one by one. I had them say their goodbyes to their grandmother as I held the phone up to her ear. I felt sad that they weren't able to say their goodbyes while she was still alive. I regretted not thinking to call each of them when I was in the ER the night before, so they could've spoken to her then, although I had spoken to my third son Josiah and he'd got to say hello and goodbye. Mom was so sweet with him: I remember her saying in garbled words, "What'ya doin?" and "I love you. Goodbye." I called my youngest son right after, but attendants had come in to wheel her out to an x-ray during the call. I didn't stop them so he could say hello and goodbye. I regretted this. But I felt that she was still with us as we said our goodbyes to her. I was sure that she was listening, and maybe watching us.

My sister looked at me and said, "she's gone". I just looked at her and tried to resettle into my feelings and proceed the way I felt I needed to be in the moment.

My sister and I talked to her and to each other. We hugged each other. We cried together. All while our older sister Connie was on the phone, being a part of it from Oregon where she and her husband had been celebrating their anniversary for the weekend. We also aided the nurse in removing all the equipment from mom. I held her hand, I told her I loved her, again, and again. It was hard to decide when to leave, even after an hour by her side. Finally, Sara said she wanted to leave to be with her husband. Did I want to leave? I wasn't sure what I wanted, but I took a deep breath and looked at mom. I gave mom a final hug, placed my cheek on hers and feel her soft warm skin on mine. I promised myself I'll never forget what this feels like: Her soft warm skin on mine in this moment.

Before we left mom's hospital room, we clipped a locket of mom's hair. We'd asked the nurse if she had a pair of scissors we could borrow. The nurse grabbed us scissors and empty tubes to place her white curls in. She was more than happy to help us with this and said that they used to do it all the time and didn't know why the materials weren't handy like they'd been before. We thanked her. Everyone in the ICU had been so great through the whole experience.

When we were finished, I hugged and kissed mom, and told her I loved her goodbye one last time. As I walked out of the room, I placed my hand on the door frame, and turned to look at her body, her face. It was hard to leave. And a part of me wanted to stay.

Sara and I made our way silently out of the hospital to where my niece had been waiting in the car. We hugged each other and cried and exchanged a few words. After our goodbyes, I walked to my car. I unlocked the car, climbed in and... just sat there, not sure what to do. What do I do now? Did I make the right choice to leave? Should I have stayed a little longer? I wanted to go back upstairs to be by her side. Just to be near her physically a little longer. I was in doubt and numb. So there I sat. Was this shock? The ferries had stopped running for the night. Do I stay at moms? No, the thought of that feels strange. Get a hotel? No, I probably wouldn't be able to sleep, and I don't have anything with me. How long until the next ferry? Around 3 hours. Do I sleep at the ferry dock? Stay on my niece's couch like she'd offered? I couldn't make a decision.

A few minutes passed and I heard a message notification. It was my half-sister in London. "Sorry I didn't respond right away yesterday, how's your mom?" I messaged back that she'd just passed, and that I'm sitting in my car in the parking lot outside the emergency room. "Do you want to talk?" she texted, then called: "I had this strong feeling to get back to you when I remembered you had messaged me. Now I know why". We talked for an hour. I know it was divinely orchestrated, and we both agreed it was exactly what I needed.

I checked the ferry schedule. Okay, only 2 hours until the next boat to Vashon. I decided to go wait at the ferry for just an hour by the time I'd get there. I promised to let my sister know when I arrive safely at home.

I wondered on the drive to the ferry: What else was divinely orchestrated today, yesterday, or the days leading up to this moment? The day before, I'd seen a Red-tailed hawk and eagle flying side by side above the highway on my way to the hospital to sit by her bedside. That was a moment I looked up and thought, that's a message. The hawk is a long-time power animal for me. The eagle entered my life in a symbolic way when it nested behind my house in 2018, and was a symbol of strength for me during a difficult time. And here I found myself in yet another difficult time of loss, and there it was to support me.

I exited the highway on the offramp to Port Orchard and sat at the stoplight. As I sat there waiting for the light to change, I found myself thinking of an idea mom had shared with us. I smiled at the thought that mom must've put that thought in my head: Months ago, she'd seen an article on Facebook about turning people's ashes into blown glass memory ornaments and keepsakes. And I remember back to when she'd suggested it to me. I remember her saying she would like that, and she'd thought it was "neat", as she'd say. I smiled, and felt as though she was with me.

I got home at around 5:00 AM, and walked into a quiet house—my boys were with their dad. I walked over to my bedside and turned on the lamp. The bulb flickered.

That hadn't happened before. I checked the bulb and lamp, and it seemed fine, so I crawled into bed. Shortly after lying down, I popped out of bed to grab my laptop. I realized lying there that I needed to clear my Calendly schedule before people could get to it. The light flickered again—three times. This was new. "This hasn't happened before," I thought....and I thought of mom. I know if I think of someone at the same time something happens it's relevant. I looked at the light, "Hello mom". It was a nice feeling that she was trying to get my attention to let me know she was near me. I was seeing signs already and this was another. I've heard many times for many years that spirits can manipulate lights. And here, now, my mom's spirit was doing it. I smiled, said "Goodnight mom," and drifted off to sleep.

Signs and support

It's Saturday afternoon, the day after her death. I reflect again on how often I've seen eagles lately. Not just flying in the sky as they naturally do. But the many times I'd seen them in "out of ordinary" situations.

One day, an eagle flew in front of my car all the way down Cove road here on Vashon Island as I headed to my son's house. It led me about a half a mile. Or while heading home a few days after that, one flew low directly over my car headed in the opposite direction. Or sideways straight over my windshield the very next day! As I sit here thinking about it, I now realize those moments were signs, because when I saw them, I thought of what eagles have come to mean to me: strength in difficult times. And in this moment, I know all together they told me that I have the strength. That Spirit is with me. That I have their support. And that I have the strength to manage my mother's death, and my grief. Will I continue to remember this? And if I forget, will I be reminded?

I also realize that I have been guided to buy things I needed for the support I need right now. I'd found an empty bottle of a tincture a friend had gifted me after my ex-husband and I had separated 4 years ago. It was a beautiful pink "heart mender" tincture. When I found the bottle I thought, "I should buy another," and did.

And when I opened the cabinet door this morning and saw it, I knew it was a gift from Spirit that I had it.

The same goes for the things sitting empty on the counter. There's the empty bottle I kept trying to remember to restock of an essential oil blend: "Console" by DoTerra for example. Or I had picked up a few extra things from the grocery store, and made a pitstop for food I didn't end up eating Friday night on the way home from the hospital: I can eat these tonight or tomorrow.

How often is it like this and we don't realize? How lovely when we do notice that these things have been undeniably set in place for us! A gift from the spirit world that wants to support us the best it can. Our loved ones, and spirit team as I call them, are on the other side supporting us. They're making sure we're taken care of in our hour of need.

Or are they glimpses that we're getting into our divine plan? That we pre-know to do this or that for an outcome we unconsciously are aware of at the time, but are unaware that this or that is coming? Either is magical. Either or both may be true.

I'm already getting signs my mother is near. Some may say it's wishful thinking, but I believe we can communicate beyond the veil. I remember having a conversation with my mother last year. I told her to communicate with me from the other side when she died, and to send me signs. I said I was open to it, and I would know it was her.

Last night, while I waited for the ferry boat, I listened to a few of her voicemail messages I'd saved on my phone. At the end of one of the messages she spoke about hummingbirds. My mother loved hummingbirds, they brought her so much joy. Hummingbirds are considered a messenger from heaven, and I wondered if she had impressed upon me to listen.

As I was thinking of hummingbirds and how much she loved them, something catches my eye. In front of me on the sun-drenched door I see the shadow of a hummingbird! Wow! I'm surprised by the sight, and delighted to see it. I look out the window for it. I just moved here 2 weeks ago and haven't put out my feeders yet. I feel that was a sign letting me know she was near, that she was okay, and still with me. I shared this experience with a friend a little later, and she said that hummingbirds connect the world of the living and the dead. Just the fact that I thought of her and hummingbirds earlier today, and then saw one, is a sign to me that she is near and trying to let me know. I guess it's time to put out my feeders so mom and I can enjoy them!

To me, none of these were coincidences—last night, my sister messaged me at the perfect time when I sat in the parking lot. When I saw the eagles last week. Seeing the red-tailed hawk and eagle flying in the sky, forming their own circles side by side over the highway. And seeing the hummingbird after thinking about mom and hummingbirds. These are not coincidences. They are messages from spirit, and this is how spirit communication works for me.

I believe our family, our loved ones, and spirit can communicate with us from the other side. They're not far. Just above us in vibration. Just a wispy fabric away from our skin. With us all the time, and guiding us along the way.

Chapter 3

Saturday Morning

I wake up. What time is it? How long have I slept? It's 9:30 AM. Four hours. I start going over everything that happened last night. I lay there, staring at nothing for a long while. I take a breath, sigh, and reach for my phone. People, friends and loved ones are checking in. I answer a few texts from friends: "Mom has passed," with a brief explanation. And while I appreciate all the condolences, I'm in a daze. I can't believe it. Every time I describe last night's occurrences it becomes more real.

My ex-husband calls, he's heard the news, and asks if I'm okay. He offered his condolences, and as I open my mouth, I start to cry. As I cry and share, he listens supportively. After I describe what happened, our conversation naturally comes to an end, and we say goodbye. My brother calls next: he doesn't know the news yet. He just knows I'd asked for prayers on Facebook for mom. We talk for a while about what happened, share some memories, and some of what's been going on in my life and in his, and say our goodbyes. A friend from back home calls to see how I'm doing. He'd kept me company on the drive to the hospital and was checking in.

A girlfriend calls. "Hey, how are you doing?". She had called me when I was on my way home from the hospital last night as well, to see how mom was doing, and how I was holding up. It was good to be able to discuss it with her and have a girlfriend's shoulder. She's had similar experiences and offers needed advice. She asks at the end of our call, "Now, what's one thing you'll do to self-care today?" This question will be with me daily from now on.

Friends are texting and I'm playing phone tag with another. It's all a whirlwind and I start blindly doing things out of habit and physical needs. The grief comes and goes. The tears come and go. My sister Connie texts, "I didn't know a person could cry so many tears." And I agree.

I miss mom already. I'm going over and over the events in my mind. Noticing things here and there. Finding myself deep in thought. I don't have much energy for anything. I coast through the day, meeting my basic needs. I stop to journal here and there, and take note of how I'm feeling. Distract myself with some tv and go back to bed for the night. The day passed rather quickly, and I don't really remember how it passed so quickly. It was such a blur.

Chapter 4

2 days later: In a daze

I blink my eyes. What is that? The foghorn wakes me. Another day. What's today? Sunday and it's quiet, except the occasional foghorn. I wonder about the time. I ask myself; how do I feel? I think on it. How do I feel? I don't know. How am I supposed to feel? I don't know. I try to pause my mind to feel. What am I thinking? What should I be thinking? How are my sisters? I think; "Am I okay with being alone?" It's nice, I think? Would it be nice to have someone here? I miss the boys. Would it be nice to have them here? I get to process. I don't have to be any certain way for anyone, nor wonder what they're thinking. I picture someone looking at me wondering how I am. I wonder about the time again and grab my phone. 9:38 AM. I see my notifications.

"How are you?" There are some pictures of mom from Vee. Vee was mom's caregiver, and they became quite close. She bonded with my mother, and felt like a daughter—which was no surprise. All our friends growing up looked at mom as their second mother. They called her Miss Connie.

The pictures are sweet. They all look happy. Mom looks happy, trying to look good for the picture. Maybe it's better for Vee than mom. Next text, "How are you feeling today?" I think to myself, I don't know. I haven't been awake long enough to know. How do I feel? Tired. I'm tired. I'm thinking, a lot. Thoughtful. I am remembering. Reminiscent. Replaying events. I don't know whether to get up or not. I'm feeling slow. "Thank you for thinking of me," I reply. Emotions well up and I cry.

The dog comes over. She's a little four-pound Chihuahua-Yorkie mix named Roxy. I pet her for a while. She's just a love and I feel that she knows I'm sad. I should get up. I should walk my lab-mix Kacey. I hear something outside—what is it? The dogs are barking. I look. Nothing going on. It's past. I think to myself, I should get someone to take care of the yard. That'd be nice. Okay, dogs.... wait, I should use the bathroom first. I'm in a daze just following my thoughts as they come. The tub looks nice. I bet that'd feel good to slip into hot water. I picture myself in the bath, lying there. Do I want to? It could get cold fast. Maybe not. I stop before the leaving the bathroom—I should brush my teeth. Okay, the dog. Let out the dog. The feeder is empty—fill it. There are dog tracks on the laundry floor, I'll mop it really quick. Next, I check on my son's pet bearded dragon I'm taking care of while he's away. I turn on it's light. Oh, you need some greens, I think to myself. I think about getting them. I head back upstairs. Open the curtains. The garden boxes outside need to be filled the rest of the way. I could call someone. I have that $60 dollars I withdrew. Is that enough? My mind wanders....

Tea. I'll make my water with tinctures. And tea. I'm out of my detox tea. Chamomile, that'd be nice. Get the water. Drip the tinctures. Heart mender tincture—I'm glad I bought it. Mushroom tincture. I wonder about a client and turkey tail tincture. Oh yeah, start the kettle. I turn on the kettle. Soup sounds nice. What soup could I make? I see mushrooms. With milk? And? Corn in the freezer, what could I do to it, do I want to make it? It could be nice to cook/make something. The bread on the counter would be good with it? Warm, I think. I could write. I should write how I'm feeling. Grab the laptop. Write a bit. Hear the kettle stop. Hear the dog bark. Listen to the clock tick. How do I feel? Should I make that soup? I'm feeling hungry already. I look at the time. It's almost 11:00 AM. That explains my hunger. I thought it was earlier. I think to myself, I should get the dog, should make that tea. I feel tired, I listen to the silence. I feel the hunger, I feel heavy.

I hear the foghorn sound loudly. Grab my phone. It's my son (they're at their dad's), "Can we fix my bracelet before Wednesday?" I type: "Yes, maybe we can do it together." Vee texts next, "Today feels like waking up from a bad dream and then realizing it's not a dream." I type, "Yes. The worst emotional hangover ever," and hit send. I haven't made that tea. I think: Can I "be there" for someone else? The thought of it makes me feel tired. Resistant. How am I feeling? I sit and stare and space out about it. It feels like at the hospital when I was sitting outside in my car staring, thinking, wondering what I was doing sitting there. "I need a feelings chart," I think to myself. No really—what is this feeling? I glance at my phone. Son texts, "Alrighty, love you". I reply, "Love you too."

Chapter 5

The beginning of the end

It was 2:30 PM on a Thursday. I was happy to have an unscheduled day. I'd slept in late. Sipped on some tea in a sunny window. Took a long bath. Listened to a talk. Received help from my son with the garden beds in the afternoon. It had been a great day and son Josiah and I were discussing possibilities for dinner. The phone rang, it was my sister. "Mom's in the hospital. They're discharging her with a bladder infection. She needs a ride home. I called Nancy but she didn't answer. You're my number two contact."

Mom is in the hospital? How'd I not know? I didn't even see anything. Hear anything. Did I get a life alert message and not see it? Why did mom call 911 for a bladder infection? It was my day off, I had the boys. Soren was at a friend's house with pick up at 4:30. The kids would go to their dad's tomorrow for five days. "Shoot, what's the ferry schedule? I don't want to go anywhere," I thought to myself. I look at Josiah. "You want to go with me?" No, he says. "Really? I don't want to leave you; you go to your dad's for 5 days tomorrow. Can you pick up your brother?" I ask. He replied, yes.

"Alright", I said to my sister, "I'm catching the next ferry".

Chapter 6

Sunday continued...

Tea. I pour my tea water. I'm hungry. Soup. I'll make the soup. Combine the two: icy corn, half of an old onion, garlic, can of cream of mushroom soup, borderline leftover glass of kid's milk. Hmm...sun dried tomatoes would be good. Maybe some cinnamon toast? I pop it down. I notice the spinach.... Feed the lizard! Recipe. "Hey Siri, corn chowder recipe."

I see a text. "I just saw your post...." Emotions are welling up. I don't have potatoes—that's okay. Toast is starting to burn, I can smell it. I look behind me, oils getting too hot. I take it off. I think, "I'm distracted." Butter the toast. Sip of tea. Do I have any regrets? Maybe not enough time spent with her in the end? We talked on the phone—was it often enough? I was busy moving all month. Had planned to see her on Sunday—today. I notice the Christmas gift I'd bought for her in Portugal. It was still wrapped, and sitting on top of the refrigerator. I'd forgotten it last time the boys and I went up to visit after Christmas. I didn't see her on Christmas. The family had decided to all do separate things this year because of covid. I remember mom saying when she called me about it: "This sucks!" And it did! I agreed with her. I didn't have the boys on Christmas. She loved Christmas. It was always her favorite holiday. I think to myself, how unfortunate to think that was our last Christmas to celebrate together. And I feel into the sting and pain of it.

I go back to chopping, and ponder: Is this grief worse or not as bad as when my ex-husband and I split? During our separation, I'd said divorce was worse than experiencing death. I'd experienced death, but was it? It was so painful. This feeling wasn't the same kind of painful though. Grief from a parent's death feels different than grief from a betrayal, loss, or my grandparents passing when I was young.

For me it feels like I'm walking through a dream. No concept of time. Just following one thought to the next. My heart is heavy. I miss her presence in my world. Most of the time I don't know how I'm feeling. I'm just being. It's a different kind of grief. Would it feel differently if I'd known she was dying and prepared for it? I had a feeling for months. Every time I saw her she seemed more frail. I wonder, how does the loss feel differently when you half expect it, or expect it, or when it's sudden? She'd been declining. I had expected it so why was I avoiding the possibility in the hospital? I didn't want to believe it, I suppose.

I start reliving the car ride to her house from the emergency room....

She said she'd told the doctor that the last few days she felt like she was going to die. I put my hand on her shoulder, "Are you going to leave us mom?" No answer. She had repeated, "I told the doctor......" 3 times! What was going on? She couldn't finish a sentence. Why? I had to tell her to start from after, "I told the doctor...."

Then there was her shaking. I asked, "Mom why are you shaking?" "I don't know," she said. "I can't control it. I shake when I'm cold I guess". "Are you cold?" I'd asked. "I think so. I'm thirsty. Where's the water?" "I'll get you some when we get to the house," I said, and I turned on the heat.

Some of her words came out jumbled. Like marbles in her mouth, or gibberish. What was causing that? And they released her!?! I guess if no family is there to tell you differently, you'd think that, at 85, she behaved that way all the time. But no. I wished I'd had more time in the hospital with her. To talk to her more. To talk to the attending nurse.

After the hospital staff had let me in to see her, I went to her bed side—in the hallway! I took her hand. Woke her up. "How are you?" She looked around as if confused. Well, I thought, I just woke her. I remembered that Connie had said she was slow to come around when she woke her up.

"Hi," she said as she lovingly held my hand and moved it tight to her stomach. She looked around. I asked, "What happened?" "I don't know," she said.

She was quiet, tired, and just wanted to sleep. I snapped a few pictures to show my sisters what I'm seeing: her confused looks. The nurse walked up. Not the attending nurse, a different one. She apologized that she'd not been available. "She's ready to go. I'll get the paperwork," she said to me. "There are a few prescriptions for her you'll have to fill. One pain reliever and one antibiotic for the bladder infection. I'll push her out. You can wait by the Emergency Room door." I told mom I'm going to get the car. She said okay. And I went and pulled my Suburban up in front of the exit.

The nurse wheeled her up to the car. Mom looked dazed. I helped her up. She was struggling to get up. Struggling to move her legs, and struggling to figure out how to get in the truck. I assisted her. Moved her body. She didn't like it. I tried to figure out how to do this. "How am I going to get you in the house if we're struggling to get you in the car, mom?" I said. The nurse was just watching. Smiling. I managed to guide her into the car and turned to the nurse: "Here is her paperwork and scripts. They hadn't called them in." I'll have to stop at the pharmacy on the way.

Mom was tired and napped in the car. She groaned every now and then. "Are you in pain mom?" She said, "No, it just makes me feel better." I remember asking this a few times on the drive to her house. I dropped the scripts at Rite Aid. I didn't want to wait for them, and she had to go to the bathroom. "I'll take you home then come back for them," I told her.

They're still there.

I pulled up to her house on an angle toward the ramp. How was I going to get her into the house? She was weak. Tired. It was hard enough getting her in the truck. Her rider? She wouldn't be able to. Her walker? We'll see. I went into the house and got the walker. Propped the door open. Brought the walker to her car door. "Okay mom, here we go, let's do this", I said. She said, "I can't" "We have to, mom; we don't have a choice. It's just you and me. We can do it together. I know you're tired. I'll help you".

I managed to get her feet on the ground. Her bottom was resting on my thigh. She held onto the walker. She was stuck, and was so weak she had issues lifting her feet to even walk. How was she going to get around her house on her own? How was I going to do this? Should I call for help? She was not going to be able to stand for much longer. She started to dip her chest and head. I tell her, "You can't do that. You've gotta keep your chest and head up. We can't end up on the ground." She said, "I can't do it!" "Okay," I tell her, "We're going to get your butt on the walker seat, and I'll push you into the house." I helped her maneuver, describing every next action, and we got her bottom on the seat. "Okay mom, I'm going to push you up the ramp. Hold on". "Don't tip me backwards", she said. She'd fallen backwards before, years ago in a parking garage. I promised I wouldn't, and said a prayer in my head. Took a deep breath. Up the driveway. Pause. Up the first level. Pause. Turned to the left. Up the second level. The wheel started to get stuck by the planter. We both startle. Breathe. "It's okay. We're good." I said. I pushed her up to the stairs. The stairs. How in the hell was I going to get her up the stairs? I thought for a minute. Is there a ramp in the back? I honestly couldn't remember. Neither could she. I didn't want to let go of the walker. I took a deep breath and told her that we're going to do this together, that I can help her stand, and she can hold onto the railing, that she could put her right arm around my neck, and I'll help her legs up. "I can't", she said, fearful. I told her, "We can do this. Okay let's go". I helped her pull herself up. "Push my butt like Connie does" she said. That was not going to work. She was having trouble standing on her own. I wondered to myself: How was she going to get around in the house? Should I call for help? Too late, we were on our way up the stairs. One leg at a time. One step at a time. Paused on each one. I'd had to help her feet onto the steps with my left foot. Guided her with my words every step of the way—just like at the hospital and getting her out of the car. She seemed so weak. What was going on? She was so fragile. So tired.

We got to the top. I had to get the walker so she could sit back down. I told her, "Don't you fall down while I'm getting this walker. Hold on." I grabbed it and successfully got her on her walker and wheeled her into the house. She'd said she had to use the bathroom, so I pushed her to the bathroom door. "Okay, here you are." "No", she says, "I can't do it." I tried to negotiate with her about it. She was upset with me. I thought: How is she going to do this if I'm not there? She had trouble keeping her eyes open. She had trouble keeping eye contact. She was stressed from moving. Her head was turned away from me like she was trying to ignore me.

"I'm tired," she said.

"Okay, let's get you to your chair then. Do you want to get into your chair?", I asked. "Sure", she says. I pushed her to her chair. She doesn't help me get her up, change her clothes, get in the chair, or stand. I thought to myself, what am I going to do? What is she going to do? There's no way she can be on her own. She can't even get off the walker. Why did they discharge her? There's something really wrong here.

I called my sister. "She's not able to do anything on her own, no eye contact, lids falling, tired, shaking, not able to finish sentences, garbled language. Did she have a stroke? What's going on?" We decide we had to call 911 for her. She was not happy about that decision and let me know. "No! Don't you dare!" she said. I sighed, told her I'm sorry, and that I have to call 911.

"911?"

"What's the problem? What are the symptoms? What's the address?"

What Is the address?!?

————

They were on their way.

When they arrived, they were the same medics who'd answered her morning call. They told me she was different than this morning when they found her on the floor. ON THE FLOOR!?! They found her on the floor!? "For how long?" I asked. "She said 24 hours", he said.

"But my sister was here yesterday. She's been confusing time this last week", I said. And we all wondered how long she was actually on the floor this morning. How'd I not know this? They asked her questions. Told me her vitals. "She's different than this morning", he said again.

The paramedics and I made a plan to get her up, to fix her clothing, get her onto the stretcher, and get her transported back to the ER—where I felt she should've stayed in the first place. I thought to myself, if only I'd had time to access mom and to speak to her more, ask questions, and ask the nurse more at the hospital... Maybe we could've avoided all this stress on mom. Was she even like this at the hospital and nobody said anything or questioned it? Did it get worse on the drive home? It was hard to say since she'd been out of it when she first woke up for about a week now. I had called her last week at 7:00 PM and she said, "Isn't it a little early to be calling me?". She'd just woken from a nap and thought it was morning instead of evening. Connie had even purchased her a large-print digital clock to help.

The paramedics and I got her clothing fixed, lifted her onto the stretcher, and into the ambulance. I kissed her forehead and told her I'd see her there. They gave me instructions before pulling out. I drove back to the emergency room.

Chapter 7

Noticing what I'll miss

I'm thinking about mom and how she'd call about things she'd seen on tv, or on the news, or about what happed that day with my sister, or at the doctor's office. I'll miss those calls. She would always do this thing where she'd be at the end of the call, saying goodbye, and then she'd add something else. You could count on it.

I've already had my first thought of, "I should call mom and tell her..." :

It was 4:24 AM on the way home on the ferry the night of her death. I was distracting myself with emails on the ferry ride home and saw I had one from Buzzsprout, my podcast hosting platform. It was an email alerting me that'd I'd had 4,000 downloads. I remember thinking, "Oh I should post about it and call mom and tell her tomorrow". I took a breath and started to cry at the thought that I wouldn't be able to do that anymore. And I wondered how often that will happen. I remember her saying that was the hardest part about losing Mommom, her mother: that she couldn't call her anymore when she had something to share.

That's going to be the hardest part for me too. Mom was my go-to when I had anything interesting or exciting to share. She was not only my mother but my friend. And it had already been hard enough that she couldn't do the things we used to do together anymore.

I thought about the new way I'll communicate with her on the other side. It's similar to how I hear spirit: it's like a thought. I'm sure it'll be the same with mom—an instant call. I've been talking to her already, so I tell her I love her, and I hope she's listening.

Chapter 8

Thank God for my sister

My sister just texted. "I've spoken with the house supervisor at St. Michaels. They gave me guidance on how to proceed. I chose cremation services; they coordinate with the supervisor to pick up mom. It will be two weeks to complete everything. The contact was nice. I told him a bit about mom to make it more personal when caring for her."

The grief hits. Back to reality. I'm so grateful I have Connie during this time—my sister is very good at organizing and making sure everything is taken care of. I find myself easily distracted right now, but she's a get-it-done type of person. She was mom's caregiver these last few months. After she'd leave mom for the day, Mom would call and say, "She's so busy. She never sits down to relax. Always doing something". And it's true. I picture her as Rosie the Riveter from the WWII *We Can Do It* poster. That's her.

I remember the thought I'd had driving to the ferry the night of mom's death. About the glass ornament keepsakes mom had loved and shared with us. In tears I text my sister back about it, and she replies, "Yes, she mentioned wanting that so it's on my list!" Perfect.

Later, I look at the date on my phone. Sunday, February 13th, Connie's anniversary. I send her a text, "Happy anniversary to you both". She replies, "40 years! Seems like a blink in time!" I feel bad for them. They'd gone to Oregon for an anniversary weekend, and had no idea what was going to happen after they left for the trip.

Chapter 9
Holding space for mom

The grief feels like a heavy weight on my body, as if I haven't slept for days. And the lack of sleep has clouded my mind. I'm in a fog most of the time. I find some distractions to temporarily give my mind something to think about, but it's fleeting. And the thoughts about mom and what I'd experienced come back in. It feels like PTSD.

I light two candles next to an angel figure on the piano in the living room. One is Our Lady Mother Mary, the other is a votive candle: one for my mother, the other to ask that my angels and guides continue to guide me. I light an incense stick, intending to bless my space, then walk into the other room.

On the refrigerator sits my mother's gift. I look at it with sadness in my heart and decide to put it next to the candles. It's still wrapped in the pretty paper the shopkeeper in Ericeira wrapped it with. I'd purchased it in a little nautical shop in Portugal the night before I flew back to the states. The two older women in the gift shop were lovely and spoke little English, me little Portuguese.

I had the gift in my purse when I drove to be beside my mother on Friday...

It was decided that I go Friday, and my younger sister would go on Saturday. The hospital allowed only one visitor per day. On the drive over, I thought about mom and how quickly things had shifted for her after I left the ER the night before.

We had received 3 calls about my mother's condition: 12:45 AM: Her lungs had filled with fluid from the IV fluids. They intubated her and sent her to the ICU. No time to call first.

3:45 AM: Her platelets were low and they wanted to give her treatment. They wanted to do more tests to pinpoint the infection and put in a central line.

9:30 AM, they asked to put a pic line in.

Friday morning *I arrived at the hospital, went through check-in at the door, then to the receptionist at the desk, then another stop to get a visitor sticker at a makeshift visitors table. I stuck it to my jacket and took the elevator to the 4th floor ICU. At the door they buzzed me in, and ushered me to her room.*

There she was on the bed. I glanced at her lying there and began to scan her from head to toe, horrified at the sight of my mother on a ventilator. I snapped pictures to send to my sisters along with an update text.

Her ankles were swollen. I thought, "Where'd she get that bruise on her toe?" And the scratches on her feet and legs? Where'd those come from?" I did not remember her new cat she'd had for a few months. Her legs were in compression cuffs. She was hooked up to multiple IV bags. There was a monitor on her right, along with the dosage regulator. The ventilator machine was to the left. This was a far cry from what I saw when I'd left late the night before.

A young man was entering data and notes into the computer. He turned and approached me, introduced himself, "Hi I'm Joe," and started to give me an update. It was almost like a foreign language and I tried to follow along so I could relay the details via text to my sisters. "When a patient has sepsis…." isn't something you wanna hear. My older sister had questioned that the night before, and I'd asked the nurse if that was a possibility.

I took a deep breath. Exhaled.

I walked over and said hello to mom, and held her hand. She did not look good. It was hard to see her this way. I watched her dreaming. What could I do? Talk to her? Give her energy work? Just hold her hand? Sit with her? Watch her breathing, animated by the ventilator?

I watched the staff and the monitor and mom's breathing.

The nurses came and went. They were all so friendly and informative and welcoming. They were doing their best to take good care of her—following protocols and whatever her monitor demanded of them. While they were doing their thing, I decided to sit at her feet and do some energy work. I held her feet. Her feet were so cold. She was running a temperature and they laid her on a cold blanket, the nurse explained. Mom wouldn't like that and I thought to myself, "I'm glad she's sedated, she was so cold yesterday. She'd hate it. I wonder if she's dreaming she's in the cold?"

I sense her energy system is low, almost nonexistent, and it just wants some gentle Reiki—a type of energy healing that's become popular and actually approved of and practiced in hospitals now. As I ran the energy, I wondered if I'm giving her energy to die. I didn't like that thought. My thoughts are how I receive information intuitively, but I tried to brush that thought aside and focus on positive healing thoughts. Sometimes a person in the dying process needs energy to pass. And Reiki—or any energy work—can assist in that process. I set aside the possibility and hoped my efforts could aid in another way. But finding my mother on a ventilator didn't give me much hope—and especially with the recent belief that the ventilator is a step towards death with people diagnosed with Covid-19.

As I held space for mom and ran energy, the staff were doing their thing: Checking the machines. Moving her every hour. The monitor went off occasionally. Her blood pressure kept dropping. They came in, assessed, and adjusted the medication. Entered notes. One time they tried adjusting her body angle to see if that might help. I told her: "Come on mom, let's regulate that blood pressure and fight whatever infection you have!" I wondered—can she hear me? It worried me that it kept dropping every few hours.

They asked for my permission before doing things. They kept me informed of everything, even the little things. The two men that came in to do the pic line were the same. Described the procedure and made casual conversation. It took hours from the time they asked about putting in the pic line to actually getting there to do it. It was successful and easy, and I wished them ease with every procedure the rest of the day as they were leaving. I texted my sisters that it was done. And made sure I relayed whatever the doctors and nurses said to me about mom and what they were doing. They still didn't know what the cause of infection is.

And they never did....

Chapter 10
Tapping into my feelings

I see a text from my sister. “How are you doing? I worry about you alone.” I reply, “I have moments I’m enjoying the peace and quiet. But not when it’s too quiet. I’m coasting.” I feel grateful to have the space to follow my grief. To go slow, to do or not do. No expectations from anyone or myself—just follow my energy and where I am in the moment.

This morning, Valentine's day, my ex-husband calls to check on me. He asks if I'd like the boys an extra day since I'd lost a day with them to go to mom. I start to cry. The thought of having them with me is more than I allowed myself to feel in the previous days. I'd missed their presence during this time and so I thank him. That was thoughtful of him. Yet strangely, at the same time, I am enjoying the time alone. I wonder, what will it be like when the boys come home? I have been checking on them every night. Asking them how they were doing. Hoping they were getting their emotional needs met. It's been hard not to have them here during this time to support them.

After the conversation, I pass by the unwrapped gift on the piano and stop to look at it. I think I may have the courage to open it. I take a picture first of it wrapped, for a memory. I pick it up and start to get emotional. I pull off the paper to reveal the nesting dolls beneath. I start to cry. I'd forgotten how pretty it is. Blue, moms favorite color, with pink flowers. I think to myself: she would've loved it had she seen it. I set it back down and snap a few more pictures to share with my sisters later.

Chapter 11

The what-ifs creep in

I wake to the sound of the heart monitor flatlining. I've been dreaming of mom's last moments and now have that sound in my head. I think to myself, I'm glad I don't have that memory, and immediately start thinking of the events leading up to her death....

Getting her in the car. How I had to help her hand onto the ceiling handle above the door. How I had to help her out of the car. Maybe if I'd called 911 then? How, in the house she'd mumbled, "No, that's where I fell, I don't want to." Sitting in the ER, how I'd helped her get some water. She was so thirsty she almost finished the whole thing. How Josiah, my 3rd son, had called, and I'd held the phone up to moms' ear. "Hello. Whatcha doin? I love you too", she said. How I'd called Soren, my youngest, right after, and how they were taking mom at the time. I should've stopped the technician so Soren could've said goodbye to her. How I'd told the nurse that she felt pain when I pressed on her stomach, and she said that her chest hurt. How I'd notice that mom said she had to pee but there was no urine in the container. And how I thought that was odd. Now I realize I should have mentioned it to the nurse—that's how she'd figured out the IV fluid was going into mom's lungs. I hadn't known that was a sign. How interesting that I'd had that thought. But I didn't know what that could've meant. Maybe if I'd mentioned it then—would it have made a difference in moms' outcome if I'd shared my thought in the ER? I don't know. They hadn't followed up on anything I said. Maybe, maybe not.

The printer just cycled itself for no reason. Interesting.

It's 12:40 PM. I drink some water, go to the bathroom, brush my teeth, walk the dog. It's been my lab Kacey's new job of guarding the door this morning and she needs to go relax. The UPS guy gave a bit of excitement. I think, I should make some food. I've been journaling this morning, and my tea has gotten cold.

Chapter 12

At the hospital Thursday night

As I sat beside her, I remembered I had mom's present in my purse. It'd been a long day by her side and I debated whether to go downstairs and get some food and stay longer, or head home for the evening. I asked the nurse what the visiting hours were—maybe I should go home and get some rest. No one had let on that there was cause for concern or that I should stay "just in case." And I felt as though there was nothing I could do but be by her side and watch the comings and goings of the hospital staff.

I started talking to her again. "Mom, you've gotta fight. You've gotta get your blood pressure under control, and clear your lungs so you don't have to be on this ventilator anymore, so we can talk to each other again. I love you."

"I have your gift here. I wish you could open it. I'd leave it but there's nowhere to put it. You need to get better so you can open it. I love you. Elan, Brennan, Josiah, and Soren send their love and say that they love you and hope you're healthy and home soon. They love you mom. Your grandkids love you. Connie and Sara both told me to tell you that they love you. The kids do too. Seth and Shaylin love you. Brita and Blake love you. Blake was going to fly home. He'll be here on Monday. Sara will be here tomorrow to see you and Connie the next day on Sunday. Did you hear me? Sara will be here tomorrow. You have to get better mom. We love you. I love you."

I stood up. I wanted to hug her but there was so much in the way. (Later I thought, I should've hugged her.) I kissed her forehead, and stroked her hair for a bit as I looked at her. Her hair was soft, silky, and a beautiful shade of white. I stared at her for a bit. I was afraid to leave. I kissed her again, told her goodbye, and that I loved her.

I stepped out and told the nurse I'm going to go. He asked if I needed anything, offered to go get me some food, and asked if I'm okay. I said I'm alright, thanked him for asking, and turned my head. The doctor had walked up to us and stood there with a concerned look on his face. I should've known. I should've read into it. He said he'd like to put a catheter in moms' arm to better read her blood pressure. I agreed and told them that my younger sister will be there tomorrow. I gave them her number, and said my older sister will be here Sunday.

I thought to myself, "I was supposed to visit mom at her house on Sunday. And here we are". I started to get choked up talking to them, then turned towards mom's room and said, "I'm just going to tell her goodbye one more time". I headed back into her room for one last goodbye, stroked her hair, and kissed her on her forehead. I left the hospital wondering if I'd made the right choice.

I remembered when I got down the stairs, I looked at the view this place had of the Olympic mountains and the water to the south. I commented to the receptionist what an amazing view she had. And thought: too bad mom couldn't see it.

Chapter 13
Navigating emotions

My two youngest sons come home today. I'm looking forward to it and watch the clock. It's been difficult not being there to support them after mom's passing—one of the things that's hard for me since starting the 50/50 parenting plan, and especially after years if being there 100% of the time for 20+ years.

I'd been checking in with them, but there's one conversation that's a standout: I'd video-called my youngest and asked him how he was doing with the grief of losing his mommom. He replied, "I wasn't that close to her." I was horrified. Why'd he feel this way? I asked why he felt that way. "Well, she wasn't nice the last time we saw her." I sighed and felt what he was talking about. On our last visit, mom wasn't well. Her filter—which, mind you, was always leaky—was gone. And she pointed out my youngest's size. Something we'd experienced growing up, but not so blatant. I immediately drew a boundary and told mom she couldn't talk to him like that without any regard to his feelings. She got defensive and snapped at me, stating her entitlement as his grandmother to say anything she wanted. I apologized to my son that day and during the conversation.

I assured him: "I'm sorry, that wasn't okay what she said. I don't condone her behavior, but Mommom wasn't in her right mind. She had started her cognitive decline and felt as if she could say anything she wanted to anyone without filter. She was sick and maybe we could excuse this one behavior. It wasn't okay, but she'd been failing. I struggled with our last visit too and I'm trying not to focus on that experience. Maybe we could give her a pass in her death process and try to focus on the previous visits—like the one where she wanted you to get off your phone and talk to her, or see the newest instrument she'd acquired, or have you play her a song on the keyboard. And it was a happier visit..." Still, though, the damage was done. My heart went out to him.

This afternoon I sat on the couch with my son and had a conversation. He wants to buy this teddy bear bouquet for his girlfriend and wanted help purchasing it. He was on one end of the couch, me on the other, facing one another. As I speak to him, I notice my hand and the way it moved, and it caught my eye. I think, "Wow, my hand looks just like mom's hand' and tears start to well. My son hugs me. And I say, "I just noticed my hand looks like mommoms". I notice as the days go by, it's the little and unexpected things that move me toward my grief.

Lately, my youngest and I hang out in my bed before it's bedtime. For some reason, my kids have felt it's a great place to hang out—choosing the comfort of my bed over the couch. I'm watching an episode of *Reign* that I binge watch on Netflix to distract myself. He calls out, "Mom, why don't you come in here with me?" So I turn off the tv and join him. We cuddle up, he on his phone, and I grab my laptop.

As we lay there, I notice the lamp flicker beside me and pause as I glance toward it. I look at the light, waiting to see if it'll happen again. Soren takes notice and pops his head up. I ask, "Mom, is that you? If so, flicker the light again". The light flickers again. Soren is amazed and joins in. We have a conversation with mom. She flickers the lamp as we ask questions. Once it even goes totally off for a second and then back on again. At the end of our conversation we both say "I love you" and the flickering stops for the night. We chat about it for a minute and snuggle up together again. He says, “That was so amazing! It’s hard to believe.”

The next day I get on the ferry and head out to meet my sisters. We’re meeting at mom’s house to assess what needs to be done, and to be together. The three of us haven’t been together since the Saturday before her death. We’d decided to meet for coffee to discuss mom’s decline and possible choices for the future when she couldn’t be alone at the house anymore. I see now what a gift the coffee date meant: it brought us together one last time before she passed.

My energy was really low last night. I didn’t sleep as well. And it feels like I’m heart sick. On the drive to the ferry I remember a time years ago: My mother and younger sister had flown out to pack up Connie and drive her from California to Maryland. Connie is 9 years older than me, and Sara 6 years younger than me. Unfortunately, dad had a gallbladder attack while they were away and had to have emergency surgery. So, mom arranged I stay at an acquaintance’s house while he was in the hospital. I was so heartsick, I got on my bike and rode all the way to the hospital in town to see dad. I remember being distant with my friend's mom and insisted that I ride up there instead of taking the drive offered. I had cried when I got to dad’s bedside and again on my ride back to the house.

My sister shares she'd awakened to a noise. Her pup raised his head to look toward the noise. She said instead of seeing mom hooked up to a ventilator like she'd been seeing her in her mind, this time when she closed her eyes she saw her lying peacefully in white clouds.

She also brought up a coincidence: The same morning, our younger sister had found a picture of us all dressed up and sent it to us (in one of those old-timey, fun, dress-up photos). She had seen that same picture earlier on her phone when she opened it as well.

A healer of mine, Aimee Traeden, said, "When we lose a loved one and we're in grief, we are more vulnerable and more able to receive communication." I love this explanation.

It was good to be with my sisters today at our mother's house. I thought it'd be emotionally difficult, but it wasn't what I'd imagined. I enjoyed being with my sisters. And it didn't feel odd to be at mom's house—it was somehow comforting, even when we got emotional a few times.

I felt cautious though—I did not want to upset my sisters or have them feel unfairness in the post-death process. So often these things can ruin relationships. I felt worried my sister wasn't satisfying her needs for fear of the same. And there was an odd sense I needed to tread lightly to not overwhelm myself.

I'm on the drive home, and I miss not riding back with them. I miss the camaraderie we had before lockdown. I miss the possibility to share our experience and lean on each other. I decide to call part way through the ride. "Did you guys see the full moon over the navy base in Gorst?" I asked. "It was huge and amazing! Just up over the horizon."

I share with them that I felt like it went well, and that it hadn't been what I expected it to be emotionally, given the difficult circumstances. We strategize the coming days.

The rest of the drive home and when I arrived home is another story. A mix of feelings start to show up: Grief, guilt, remorse, confusion. I reflect on the afternoon. What started out slow and reverent had started to feel rushed and overwhelming, unreal. I was left questioning my experience. Had I been ready? Was it too soon? Were there unsaid expectations? Was there anything my sisters weren't expressing? Was someone not speaking up? Should we have just made a plan?
And this was after only 5 hours, two grocery bags and one bin's worth! What would it continue to feel like as we slowly sift through the rest of her house? Each room is easily a day's work. All this is equally confusing and emotionally stirring. I take a deep breath and try to settle my mind.

Chapter 14
Lyric Messages

I woke this morning to a line of a song in my head. It was from Edwin McCain's, *I'll Be*. The line says, "…the greatest fan of your life", and it was on repeat. At first, I thought I heard, "…the greatest man of your life." Haha. But then I recognized the tune behind it. Yesterday, it was another song snippet repeating as I woke up, "…a new relationship…." from the Usher song, *You make me wanna*. I regularly follow my dreams, dissect their meaning, and keep a journal. I lay in bed with the song lyrics repeating in my head and wonder about the message, and if mom's playing a roll. As soon as I have the thought, I know that thought to be true. I know that whenever a person pops into my mind when I'm thinking of something, it's related—especially with a deceased loved one.

I know that when I see something, and it sparks a memory, and then a thought follows, it's usually my own memories and thoughts being triggered. But when I hear a song, or see a butterfly or hummingbird, or find a penny and then think of a departed loved one, it's them giving me a message. So, I reflect on and contemplate the possibilities.

I often get songs as messages. One day I was driving to pick up my son from soccer practice. Out of nowhere my phone in my purse started to play a song from the 90's I hadn't listened to in ages by Kenny Wayne Shepard. It was a song about having one foot in the door and one foot out. On the way home, my son and I stopped into a local burger spot to grab some food, and the same song started to play over the speakers. I couldn't believe it! What are the odds! I knew it was a message but didn't understand until a few months later.

The lyrics I received were messages from mom. Mom was my biggest fan. And mom and I are beginning a new type of relationship together. In this situation, if I look at just the line repeated, it's simple to see she's using the words of the song to say something to me. If Spirit were communicating something to me and I heard a song, I may want to listen to the whole song to try to figure out the meaning. As with that 90's song: there was more to the message upon reading the lyrics. When our departed loved ones want to relay a message to us, it comes in the words needed to get the message through, including one phrase or a grouping of words repeating in your mind.

As I contemplate about mom's death and the grief that accompanies it, it's comforting to know that she's trying so hard to reach out from the afterlife. It's so hard to feel that she's gone, and that her physical presence isn't in my life. Yet she wants to let me know she's still around.

Death and loss play a huge role in our lives—we've all experienced it. Some at a young age, and some don't experience it until later in life.

I was 6 when I lost my grandparents, who were like second parents to me. I've always felt like my grandmother was a guardian of mine. And I know my mother is with her and my great grandmother. I could feel them there in the ER that day.

After my biological father's' suicide around my 18th birthday, I'd felt disappointed that I never got to meet him. And I'd not really sensed any communication from him after his passing.

But after my half- sister Darlene's death in 2016, she sent hearts and messages to our sister and me. She would ring the phone at midnight when I had a land line.

I tried to debunk it. One night, she even used my brother-in-law's phone to FaceTime me at 3 AM. And he didn't even have my number! I still wonder what would've happened had I answered. She had been very present after her death up until I felt her communication start to fade a few years ago. I feel as though when they acclimate to the other side, the occurrence of signs and messages starts to fade.

Chapter 15

What I could do…but can't

I'm tired. I woke up too early. I spent an hour looking for a song I'd heard last week on the way to and from the hospital. I should've gone back to sleep after my sons left for school this morning. Why didn't I? It's almost noon and I've just had tea and a few pieces of raisin bread. I think to myself, "I need to get my eating in check. I've been emotionally eating. This counts as intermittent fasting, right?!? "Don't eat late!!" Will I succeed? I don't know. I booked a weeklong getaway yesterday afternoon with Alaska's $99 each way fare sale to Hawaii. It'll be good to get away alone, and do exactly what I'm doing now but on the beach. Maybe set a goal. I think to myself, "Maybe a 30-day Instagram stretching challenge?" It'll help me be disciplined. Hmmm, maybe not. Seems overwhelming right now. Would I even be able to do it every day? Better not to push myself. I decide to continue to follow the grief.

A good song plays on my phone. I'm soaking in the tub. I'm numb. Trying to feel, but too tired. It's a good song and my thoughts go into auto pilot. I picture myself dancing. I haven't gotten on my pole in a long time or done a pole dance class in forever. Maybe that? Where to put it? It's not up yet since moving. My new place is small and there's no room upstairs. Basement?

I picture myself dancing. Then picture the service guys seeing it Monday. No, maybe after. I'm tired. "Could I even do it?" I think to myself.

I picture all these things "I could do" but feel like I don't have the energy or that they're not even possible right now. Stretching? Dance? Yoga? All seem like effort. I'm too tired. I would probably feel good though….

But instead I give myself a pass, and think to myself, "Things will shift," and remember back 4 years ago: I'd been in a state of grief, post-separation, and had felt my grief shift one morning 3 months later. It was the beginning of spring. I wonder to myself, how long before I feel better?

I remember my youngest Soren had asked yesterday if I'd had any communication from Mom. I contemplated for a minute. Had I? Maybe a little thing here and there that reminded me of mom. Sweet that he had asked. It's comforting to see little possibilities hinting that she may be around. I know he had enjoyed the flickering light experience.

I think to myself, "Should I post for my business today on social?" I try to think of something, but it all sounds uninspiring.

A few texts come in. Sister: "Good news. Shaylin just got a job at Boeing." Then a funny video from a friend I can't hear. I text, "I can't hear the video." There's a comment on a picture I'd sent as I share my excitement for my niece....

I take a deep breath and go back to trying to relax.......

It's funny how life just "continues on" while you're in your grief. I experienced that after a fire we'd had in late August 2011. We lost nearly everything. It was devastating. And while I grieved the loss, I realized the world continued to spin. Life happened whether I was a participant or not, with or without me. And life will be there when I return.

Chapter 16
Clairaudient messages

I heard mom's voice as I drifted off to sleep last night. I'd forgotten about it until just now. It surprised me as I'd become conscious of what had just happened, and realized it was her voice. I heard "her" voice say, "Lisbeth" quite clearly, like a whisper. I was in that state in-between awake and asleep. Robert Moss calls it the hypnogogic state: a state you can reach not only before dropping into or out of sleep, but also in meditation. It's a space accessible to spirit for communication since the conscious mind has let go. The discipline is to stay in that space to continue the dialogue or be able to listen. Whenever I hear these voices, though, my conscious mind always grasps onto them, and I lose the connection.

In late 2017 I was driving across the West Seattle bridge to the Fauntleroy ferry dock one night. I was on my way home from a yoga meditation course I'd been taking from East West bookshop in Seattle. I was spacing out on the drive and heard, "Are you ready?" It was a man's voice, and it took me by surprise. I popped right out of that in-between space where you're driving on auto pilot, spacing out in deep thought or contemplation or daydream. Probably a good thing, since I was driving, ha-ha. But that's the space I'm referring to: just one example of spirit being able to speak to you when you get out of the way.

This evening another song pops into my head as I laid my head on the pillow. Again, it's not the whole song. It's always just a few words. This time it was, "I'm sorry that I let you down", from the song *Let You Down.* by NF. I love how mom is using this way of communication to speak with me. I understand it and it's working. I'm receiving the messages. They give us the messages in a way we can receive them. And these lyrics make sense to me. To anyone else it could easily be chalked up to an earworm (when a song gets stuck in your head), but I'd not heard it that day. And the same is the case for all the other song words I've been thinking this week. It's clear to me this is one of the ways she's choosing to communicate.

Another example of when spirit was communicating with me: I was driving to meet a friend for a walk and chat. On the drive, right before I got to the trail, the song *Talk* by Khalid started playing over the radio saying, "Can we just talk?" It's funny how often this happens when you start to pay attention. A coincidence? No.

Chapter 17
Loss is an Initiation

I got a reading and energetic home clearing last Tuesday from a seer and healer named Aimee Traeden. My friend Allison had shared her contact information with me last year when I'd needed to clear excess energies still left over from my divorce. Aimee is great, and always right on. Two weeks ago, I'd called her asking for a session to clear the house and property I'd just moved into last month. I'd been having nightmares and wasn't settled into the new property just yet. And I'd been feeling and seeing the past renters leftover energy around the area. I feel it's always good to get assistance even if I've been doing my own clearing—especially when I may be energetically connected to a space or person. We scheduled a chat for this past Monday.

After a brief discussion about my desires, she scheduled the remote reading for the next day, last Tuesday.

In the recording she mentioned she'd seen an overall theme of an altar (a spread of objects and different cards and things) she had created for the reading; and the theme resonated with me. I've spoken about it in my work—initiations. As we go through life, initiations are events and processes that can radically change us and our lives because they force us into personal growth or creative momentum. Examples of these are births, deaths, accidents, illnesses, and tragedies.

In my reading I loved what she shared about loss and initiation. She said, "With the passing of your mother, and your move, you have been going through a kind of initiation. Stepping into something new. The card, four of wands, has a hummingbird on the top, and I thought of your mom. It represents celebrating an initiate, a crossing over. So for women that can be: getting your period, or having a baby—a momentum, a big step in life. An initiation through that experience, and the women in your life who are supporting you through that. Losing your mother is an initiation. "We all will experience loss, we will all lose someone in this way, it's part of the process of life. We come, we grow, we die. We will all eventually lose a loved one. Feeling the initiation of what it's like to feel the loss of your mother, and the compassion you gain. Which is a big shift that changes your life forever. And at the same time the energy of your altar is that even the grief process puts you in an altered state. And even though you have all the emotions that come with that, grief is also an empowered state. Altering in consciousness. To find a sense of balance, to step into your full ability, to find and live a beautiful life. Can you connect to the beauty you find in life to help you heal? That, with the move which is also a loss; You're being asked to look at life through a new lens".

Chapter 18
Part of the process(ing)

Week two. I'm starting to feel like I'm coming out of the fog. I still feel tender though, and I know being around people would be overwhelming. My energy is low and I'm tired, but lighter in a way. I have more of a slightly distracted mind rather than a fully consumed mind.

I still flash back to the emergency room. The house. The night back in the ER. Going over things, putting the pieces together; or trying to. It's hard not knowing the cause of death. What stands out is that it was so fast.

Reports are starting to come back, but still no answers. I'm trying to find resolve in the "not knowing". Trying to wrap my head around, "it was just her time." Or "She chose to go." Trying to find some peace in knowing she's not in pain anymore. She's with family, and friends, and those she touched in life, and who touched her.

It's actually been fun to think of the people from her past who have crossed over and I wonder, "Maybe they're hanging out on the other side together now, reconnecting." Or, "Maybe she's in the arms of a past lover". Nice to think that she's with the spirit family I saw surrounding her hospital bed. My grandmother and great grandmother. The ones on the other side who I heard say, "We've got her." Knowing they've got her now brings me some peace.

I'm on the road. Driving is always a good time for me to clear my head. Think-itate on things, so to speak. My older sister and I are meeting at mom's today. There's much to do to clear out twenty plus years of things around the house. And there's so much from her past that she'd brought from the East coast across country. Many years of life under one roof: Her parents, her marriages, her single time.

Craft projects started. Many projects in waiting. Old projects never done. Mom was so talented and always up to something crafty, sometimes moving into another project without finishing the last. Well, at least that's what it seems from the knitting projects that have been found here and there. And the undone projects awaiting attention.

She was just tired at the end. She'd have a great idea and not be able to do it or have the energy to attempt it. I'm sure that was difficult for her— she was fiercely independent in that arena. I used to watch in wonder at the many projects she and dad tackled over the years. They were well matched in that way—clever and crafty, and quite capable. Always busy!

But not this last year. The spark just wasn't there. Her motivation dwindled. Age caught up to her. She often said how tired she was, and that her body stopped cooperating with what her mind wanted to accomplish. I'm sure it was frustrating for her to see her own energy level decreasing these last few years, and not be able to do the things she used to do.

She'd spoken to us about how she felt like her time was limited. How she felt like she didn't have much time left in her life. How she was eager to spend time with us because she felt each time she saw us may be the last.

Seven months ago, last July, she'd had a fall which gave her a pretty serious concussion. She'd fallen in the kitchen from a dizzy spell and hit her head. My sister had found her the next day. I feel that was really the start of the downhill journey.

At mom's, my sister Connie and I start in the living room. Mom has a curio case with her figurines in it that sat behind her lounge chair which doubled as a bed. My older sister and I were looking at them, sorting through them, deciding which ones to keep, who wants which, and which ones would go. We noticed the one I'd given her that I'd found at a local Goodwill. A Lladro of a young girl holding a stuffed toy. But the one I'd given her had a broken hand. The one in the case did not. Interesting.

Later that afternoon I found the original one on a dresser in an upstairs bedroom. Funny. I suppose she loved it so much she'd wanted to have an unbroken one like it? Mom. I don't know. I'll never know. It's been fascinating to realize things as we clean and pack and sort. Each item takes us to a specific memory or time. This part of the process brings up a lot of emotion, and I feel it is an integral part in the grieving and healing process.

I remember when I was in my four-year healing program. My teacher had spoken of her own mother's death, giving us a glimpse into her process. She'd shared how she'd gone to the morgue and cleaned and dressed her mother. How it was important for her to do so. And how healing that was for her. So often these days in society we have things in place to save us from such moments we think we may not want to experience. But these moments could have so much gold in them for us and our healing process. They can help us to find closure and to say goodbye.

Chapter 19
Her urn

My sister sent us a text message today. It was a picture of an urn. It's almost like it was made for her. A beautiful dark blue with a flower sprig and a hummingbird. She loved blue. Everything in her house for years, since I can remember, has been a colonial blue. Sometimes accents of a darker blue. Antique China, Delph, Dutch plates and vases, flowered curtains and China, figurines; all blue. Picture a white background and the blue pictures, accents, and flowers. Intermixed with solid blue furniture, and her antique early American wood furniture. And the hummingbird! I text back, "That's so pretty, I think it's perfect."

Chapter 20
The dimensions of grief

My older sister and I are back at moms again. Two days of sorting and packing. It's nice to spend time together and share memories. We find pictures here and there, next to special things she had, and inside books, magazines, and boxes. We find recipes, and notes she'd written and tucked away. Pictures of things she owned or wanted to make or had already made. We talk and tell stories and wonder about things together, laugh and share the experience. I've appreciated the time to be in mom's space, and share the experience with my sister as we support each other. I wouldn't trade this precious time for anything.

The second day on the way to mom's I'd had time to stop. I pumped some gas, and ran into Safeway for a few items for home; soup for dinner, some light bulbs, a drink. When I walked through the store I got flooded with emotion and sadness. All of a sudden I was overwhelmed. I felt like I was in the way, or others were in my space. I didn't know whether or not I could manage. I wandered through the store not being able to think about if I needed anything extra than what I'd gone in for. Just passing by the items and shelves and aisles in a state of unknowing. I was surprised at the feelings of sadness I'd felt. I thought to myself, "In the grocery store? Why here?"

When I arrived at mom's, I shared this with my sister, and she said she'd had the same thing happen. Was it that we shared memories of mom there? There were days we'd taken her to the store or when Connie picked up orders for her. The memories of when we were children or adults and how she'd say way too much to the cashiers when we were there? Was it just that the busy store was too much for my sensitive energy system? Maybe all the above.

It was a full weekend, including the hour and a half to and from mom's. I didn't realize until afterwards the toll it took on my system. By the end of the weekend, I was really feeling it. Sunday evening, when I arrived home, I settled in with some warm soup I'd grabbed at Safeway, and reflected on the day.

The following day, I was drained. I was so tired I spent the day just laying around. No energy to do much but contemplate the weekend, take care of myself, and distract myself with some Netflix. My sister and I texted about odds and ends and shared how nice it is to spend time together. I'm glad we have each other.

I've been surprised at what I can't handle. Even the thought of doing something seems overwhelming at times. I can usually zone out any chaos—but not in this state. I feel a fragility, a tenderness that's sensitive to the touch, to anything that may be too much. And then on other days I'm just fine. I get a burst of energy to do my podcast, have a client, or tackle a box or 2 left over from my move or mom's. It comes and it goes just like the sadness and grief.

My grief experience is multidimensional—affecting me on all levels: Physically, mentally, emotionally, energetically. After the initial shock of her death and the days just after, it's a coming and going. Recently, I've begun to notice that my grief is triggered by things. Yes, I still wake with her death on my mind some mornings, but most of the time it just hits me when It's triggered by random things.

My sister mentioned that after she lost her dad she had the childhood show *The Chipmunks* trigger an emotional response. Last night a friend who'd lost her mother at the end of last year shared how she'd had a purse of her mother's on her arm the other day. When it touched her hand, it was like her mother was holding her hand, and that it'd moved her to tears.

Random triggers: Me in Safeway. A thought about Hawaii and how she said she'd wanted me to take her this year. Last night watching the last episode of the show *1883,* I cried through the whole thing.

Chapter 21
The gifts of loss

During my divorce process I became aware that grief has its own trajectory. There's no timetable. For some it seems it can be short, and for others, long and seemingly unending. I believe my own mother had the latter. She told stories of her hurts and pain and losses well into her 80's. I feel if we try to suppress our grief, or deny it, it will just prolong the process. Or it will cause physical pain in our bodies. I'd witnessed it in my mother's body, how stuck emotional pain can be seen in the body after time, and even cause dis-ease in the physical and emotional bodies.

Observing my mother, she had always been a motivator for me to work on my own emotions and personal processes.

In my late 20's it was my anxiety and panic attacks shortly after saying "I do" that led me to the four-year healing school. And I often see in my healing clients how our emotions can settle in the body and cause dis-ease when not processed out. Our energy system has the ability to hold onto everything we experience. With each experience, there's the possibility to do harm if not dealt with.

Along with being an Intuitive healer, I'm also a podcast host. One of my recent podcast guests was author and coach Lolita E. Walker. After posting her episode on Instagram, she wrote, "May we lean into our momentary interruptions and shift to our greater selves." A great reminder that in these difficult moments in our lives there are gifts available to us. She calls these moments of loss and diversity "momentary interruptions." She explains that, in these moments, "...it's up to us to choose if and how this thread will weave into our lives." She stated that we can use the moments which have pressed the pause button on our lives to move us forward. And it's so true!

I've experienced this on many occasions. A car accident at 21 would eventually put me on my healer's path. The panic attacks I'd mentioned earlier put me into the four-year healing program. It was my marriage dissolution that propelled me into self-empowerment in a new way, to get serious about my healing practice, to start my radio show, to ease my fear of public speaking, and subsequently to start my podcast. So much good came out of these losses!

So how is this moment in time moving me forward? The grief is so different than the loss of my marriage. The loss of my mother is a tender feeling pain, where the divorce was heart breaking. This is more of a heart ache, the divorce more triggering of past core wounds around abandonment. This isn't abandonment, it's pure loss. This brings me into that feeling of an initiation into mother-lessness, and a deeper sense of compassion. The loss of the nurturer in my life, and of the friend she'd become is less of an egoic loss, and more of a heart centered loss. Perhaps this is an invitation to step more fully into my self-nurturing and self-loving. And it's an invitation to bring my sisters in closer and strengthen our bond. And to seek out support in other ways, because she was my go-to person. I now find myself rethinking my relationships and their meaning in my life. I'm rethinking the support structures in my life and what I want those to look like in the future. And I'm wondering how I might create that support.

Chapter 22
Energy and the afterlife

It's been 2 ½ weeks since mom crossed over. I started taking clients again in my healing practice this week. It's also been nice to do a few podcast recordings since moms' passing. Nice to feel that I have enough energy to serve again. It's not a full workload, mind you—just one or two things this week. Any more would be pushing my energy system, and I can feel after working with a client that one client was my limit, and any more than a few per week would be too much.

A regular client of mine arrived at his 11:00 AM appointment. I've been working with them for some time. I always set up sacred space before a client arrives. I light a candle and ask the universe, "...for my client's spirit team and my spirit team be present for this healing. That spirit channel through me the healing needed for the highest and best outcome for everyone involved”. This time, I added, “Spirit please carry my grief while I’m with my client”.

It was an interesting experience. As I tapped into the energy I felt from the client, I noticed it was like the energy I’d felt while giving my mother Reiki in the hospital on that Friday afternoon. At that time, I had no knowing she was going to pass. Nor did I have any prior pre-death experience, or worked on someone under sedation. My intuition told me that what I felt while working on my mother was a low energy and the sedation. I remember praying for a turn in her condition and hoping for the best outcome. Being related to my mother, it was always hard to keep my personal desires around the outcome of energy work out of the healing.

I come back to my client and sink into the feeling. I check in on myself. Was I not running energy as usual? Was it too soon to take clients again? I sink in and check in again. No, I’m connected. I feel grounded, present. I check in with his energy system. It was an almost “not there” type of feeling. What was this lack of presence I felt? As I work on my client, I access the energy. Slow…low…not present…detached…? Knowing they had an upcoming procedure the following week, I start to work with them on being present in their body, embodied and grounded.

Part of my process is releasing any attachment to an outcome, and I continue the healing.

After the healing, I asked them how they felt about the upcoming surgical procedure. They shared that before a procedure they're always faced with their own mortality. And, when working with me, they always get communication from their ancestors—they've showed up telling them how stubborn they are, and how that's how they've defeated the odds.

After my client, I clean up and clear the space. I'm left questioning the feeling (or lack thereof) and put it in my knowing for future experiences. We have the choice whether to be present in our bodies or not. We have the choice to be on this planet or not. Sometimes our energy is low because we're drained or disconnected. Sometimes our energy is low, and we can decide to rally. Sometimes our energy is low because we're deciding to exit. In mom's case, she had decided that was her exit point. Her energy system was collapsing, and she was passing on. It's up to us, nature, and the strength of our bodies in any given moment what our choices may be.

Post client, I stand at the kitchen sink, look out the window, and start to daydream about being with mom at the Emergency room. How she was. My experience there. Had I known then? Had I chosen denial, because I did not want to face the possibility that was the end? I start to hear a song by Sarah McLachlan in my head. "I will remember you .." repeats in my mind. I see mom in my mind and know it's her.

The other night I was listening to a talk about mediumistic skills with mediums John Holland and Janet Nohavec. They're a few teachers I've been learning from as this skill is reopening in me these last few years. In a part of the talk they spoke about clairaudience. That when you hear song lyrics or part of a song, that's a message and it's your clairaudience. My clairaudience is one of the main ways my mother has been communicating with me. Song lyrics, hearing my name the other night, a toning in my left ear. My strongest sixth senses are claircognizance and clairvoyance, but I also sense with the other "clairs" in varying degrees, like many other psychics and mediums. It's been interesting, I feel like I'm honing my clairaudience skill in communication with mom. I'm getting the chance to practice it and learn more about how I receive in this way. I know the song lyrics I've received since her death are one of mom's ways of communicating with me from beyond.

Later that evening, I got the idea to do a memorial video with the song. Recently I'd seen one on social media a friend of mine had posted for his father and thought it was a sweet way to pay tribute to him. So, I made a video for my sisters and myself and sent it to them. I think mom would approve and think to myself, she probably planted the idea in my head since it popped in a few times that evening to do it. I cried through the whole thing. It was a sweet way to do a little memorial and show her I love her.

I also feel that mom has been communicating with me in my dreams. I'm not seeing her in my dreams, but my last few dreams I think are about her life. At first I thought one was about my sisters and I, because there were 3 women in the dream. But with further dissection of my dream, I think there can be multiple meanings.

In the first dream I dreamt there were three different stations, each one had a woman and a poisonous snake. The first woman was bit on the toe and the doctor couldn't save her. The second woman was bit on the hand and the doctor saved her. The third woman caught the snake's head so it wouldn't bite her.

As I contemplated this dream throughout the day, I didn't know if this was about me and my two sisters, or my own life, or my mother's life. It could be interpreted either way. In the first possibility it could be how each of us is handling the aftermath of moms' death. In the second interpretation it could be my past relationships. But after looking up dream interpretation and hearing a discussion on dream symbolism, I think it's showing me my mothers' life with her three husbands.

The overall feeling of the dream was fear. The snakes usually represent masculine energy. The hands are your will. And your feet are your path in life. So, if I look at the first woman, she's been bitten on her toe, which is her life's path. During mom's first marriage, she gave up her nursing career to be a stay-at-home mom. The second woman got bit on the hand and survived. Mom had given up her will in her brief second marriage but survived it. And the third woman was fighting to capture the snake. Mom fought for her independence in her third marriage, started her dance school ,and stood up for what she wanted—or took what she wanted.

The night before, I dreamt of a woman who picked out a beautiful sapphire evening dress. It was a V-neck, vintage shantung silk, A-line, size 0. She held it up to herself and chose to try it on. When in the dressing room she had chunky heels with ankle straps she struggled to remove, and panty hose on. It was all very 50's looking—especially the size and shape of that dress! When she went to try on the dress it was gone. So were her clothes. She was in a panic because she couldn't find her things. The woman ran outside asking for help, repeating, "I can't find my clothes. Can you help me find my things?" and got locked out. Before I woke she was banging on the door saying "Let me in!" And she couldn't get into the house.

I believe this was also mom. I'd spoken with mom this last year and told her she needed to heal and let go of things. That if she didn't, she'd take everything into her afterlife and the next one. Maybe the dream of the scenes was her way of showing me she was working on things, or showing me in a dream what had happened.

My sister Connie and I have been packing moms' things recently. Was she trying to ask me in the dream where all her things had gone? Was she showing me how she was feeling? Was she confused and didn't know where they had gone? I'd been questioning if being sedated at her death may have affected her transition. Could she had been confused about her death even though I know her grandmother and mother were there in her afterlife to help her? Could that be the case? Uncertain, I decide to talk to my angels and guides, and hers, and ask them to help my mother if she needs it.

I decide to talk to her. I wonder if she's listening or if I even need to worry about this. I continue anyway. I describe her death experience, what had happened in the hospital, tell her that she'd passed away, and to look for the light. That she could still communicate with us in the afterlife after she'd gone into the light. And I pray for my family to guide and help her along her journey.

I wonder though, because let's be honest, we don't really know. I don't "really" know. I decide I'll ask again before falling to sleep tonight. "Show me what I need to know". And I wait for an answer.

Chapter 23

Podcast synchronicity

I was thinking about my podcast and how the shows that were scheduled around mom's passing have lined up with my experience. I don't think it's a coincidence. Before mom's death, I had interviewed Lolita E. Walker about how life change can move us forward. And world known opera singer/sound healer Jeralyn Glass started spirit communication with her deceased son after he'd passed. She shared her journey through the experience with him which continues today.

After mom's death, Kevin Todeschi's interview about the Akashic Records, Dawn-Renee Rice about parenting, and Robert Waggoner's interview about lucid dreams were on my schedule. Each one was a gift of healing for me in one way or another. Each one had a little this or that around healing, life or after life, relationship, or spirit communication—exactly what I needed during my grief process.

Lolita's interview offered a way to take charge of my experience post life-changing event. Dawn's offered a perspective on parenting and the difficulties of being a mother while I contemplated my own relationship with my mother, her parenting style and my own. Robert's offered a glimpse into spirit communication through dreams. And Kevin told many stories about the vast possibilities we have in this life, and how we can access all timelines past, present, and future at any time.

Each one gave me a jewel I can use for my own healing process. This also shows me once again how the universe is always conspiring to help us along our journeys in life, whether we are aware of it or not.

Chapter 24
Soul family

Before my podcast this morning I went over to the piano to light the candles and call in my guides and angels. I also lit a candle for my mother at the little altar I created for her, also on the piano. I noticed when I lit the candle that she didn't feel present like before. I questioned if she was even around, and it really felt like a no. I wondered if the previous work I'd done had shifted the energy around her death state. I went about clearing for the interview. That was at 10:15 AM.

A few hours later, I headed over to the Korean spa in Tacoma on the 12:10 ferry. I love this spa, it's a real special space for women. On the way there, I get a text from my ex-husband that my ex-stepson and his wife had welcomed their second daughter into the world. In all the chaos of having to find a new rental, pack the house and move and mom's passing, I'd totally forgotten about the expectant parents and when their due date was. Since the divorce, my boys usually keep me in the loop about their step-siblings. And it dawns on me why I hadn't felt mom this morning. I believe a spirit goes wherever they are needed. And she loved my now ex-stepson, so of course she'd be there.

It's funny, this past week I'd had three different conversations around reincarnation and mom. I joked with my older sister how the psychic Silvia Brown had told everyone in her family not to get pregnant or have a baby after her mother died so she wouldn't reincarnate back into the family too soon. I had told my son Josiah that if anyone in the family had a baby or got pregnant there was a chance mom could possibly reincarnate back into the family. And it came up on a walk with a girlfriend this past Saturday as well. How fun would that be if she reincarnated as their daughter. Their daughter's name means blue in another language. Mom's love for blue—that would be a perfect name for her reincarnated self!

I believe there are soul families—souls reincarnating into different roles with each other throughout many lifetimes together. I often wonder if my younger sister is part of my grandmothers' soul. Before my grandmother had passed, she'd told my mother she was pregnant and going to have a girl in April. Mom assured her she was not pregnant. But my sister was born on April 27th. And, I have personally felt many of the souls in my family pre-birth—they hang out over my right shoulder before they've incarnated.

So maybe mom or a part of mom's soul has decided to incarnate again? It would make sense. She loved my ex-stepson, and it's still in the soul family. Or maybe I hadn't felt her around because she'd gone off to be with them during their birth process. Or both. But how fun would it be if she has incarnated, and if she ended up being one of those children who can remember their previous life—and says hello.

Chapter 25

Hearing, sensing, seeing

Last night, before I fell asleep, I'd asked my mom to give me a sign that she was still around. I'd listened to a *sitting in the power* meditation while I was on the 15-minute ferry boat ride home. *Sitting in the power* is a type of meditation that's used to connect you with universal and divine energy. It allows your vibration to increase, and your energy becomes higher and lighter, enabling you to connect with the spirit world. During the meditation, I sensed her with me. I listened in a little further and asked myself if she was with family: Mommom and Nahmaw, her mother and grandmother. I could feel them behind me, see them and hear them all giggling in my mind's eye.

When I woke up this morning, I heard a few words from a song. “Sister and your mom”, with the tune behind it. I looked up the song. It was *Abcdefu* by Gayle. I know the message was just the words, “sister and your mom”. But I listened to the song and laugh-cried all the way through it. It was too funny! I said out loud, “Love you mom!” and smiled, still chuckling to myself. Then I texted my sisters to share.

Clairaudience is a way our spirit guides, angels, and loved ones can communicate with us. Through our psychic sense of hearing, we can receive guidance and have a two-way conversation with those not in the physical form. The song lyrics and the laughter I’d heard is clairaudience. The feeling I had that they were beside and behind me is clairsentience. And the sight of them in my minds eye is clairvoyance. I feel so grateful that I’m able to have this newfound relationship with my mother. I know that life doesn’t end, that we don’t just “die”. I know that our energy, our spirit, our soul continues in a new way outside the physical and that we’re able to continue our relationship in a new way from beyond the veil.

Chapter 26

Packing, planes, and automobiles

It's early morning. I have to catch a 4:00 PM flight to Maryland later today. My younger two sons and I catch an early boat over to my mom's house to load up the Suburban with the last of the things I need to grab from her house before I leave town. I'm leaving to visit dad for a few days. I'd made the reservations a few weeks ago when a $49 sale from Alaska hit my email box. It really felt like a great idea at the time to visit him and spend some time with him. I had thought that four weeks since moms' passing would be enough time. Boy, does time fly!

I arrive at mom's house with the boys. We start to fill up my car with the last of the heavy things still needing to be moved, as well as a few leftover odds and ends. My older sister is just a few minutes behind me. She's on her way to fill up her truck as well. It'll be good that the boys and I are there to help her. She and my brother-in-law are wanting to do some moving while I'm gone and I've felt bad I won't be around to help. It's good I can help her in this moment. Because I'd underestimated that it would only take four weeks to go through mom's house, I didn't anticipate being unavailable for her.

She arrives and we hug, say our hellos and get to work. After we finish loading everything, we have a little small talk before we go our separate ways again. We both mention to each other we're tired. She mentions that she's been waking up around 3:00 AM every night. I have been too. "No way, me too," I say. And we both say at the same time, "it must be mom." My half-sister has been in this space already. Her father passed not too long ago and she has some reference point to the grief and afterlife process. I've appreciated her insight and transparency into her past experiences.

3:00 AM is considered the witching hour—the time of night that spirit is most active and can bridge the gap easily between worlds. Connie goes on to say that she isn't feeling her around like before. I agree, and say I'd felt the same. I continue by telling her about my dream of the blue dress. We wonder together how mom is doing with her transition in the afterlife. I think to myself, "Wouldn't it be nice if we could play a role in the transition?"

After our conversation, we say our goodbyes and the boys and I head for the Bainbridge ferry to get to the airport.

On the flight I'm sitting next to a man and his son. They're going to Washington D.C. for his uncle's memorial. He's passed during covid lockdown and the family was gathering there to finally have the service. His uncle had served 30 years in the military, with 2 purple hearts and another award that escapes me. He's proud. He himself had served 5 years in the marines and had retired when his son was born.

There's no coincidence that I sat next to him having just lost my mother a month ago almost to the day. Funny how that works. We have a great conversation, then both settle into the four-hour plane ride to Maryland. We share our good wishes to each other when we part ways.

I head to the car rental facility. I feel good about the flight, the conversation, the interaction, and the good vibes. I'm grateful to have had someone next to me with good energy—always a plus as an empath, haha. Plus, I think I'm glowing with anticipation to see my dad because the car rental guy upgrades me for no apparent reason. I'm both surprised and grateful, so I thank him and head toward the peninsula of Maryland.

I turn on the radio: DC 101. How fun to be hearing songs of my past in the area of my past. The beltway is a familiar drive, having taken it on my way to Casanova,

Virginia when I lived there for two years in my early 20's. To my surprise, *Lightning Strikes* starts playing on the radio! Had I not just written that down a few weeks earlier? A definite sign mom is with me on my journey home. It's meant to be, there are no coincidences.

Chapter 27
Connection

It's good to be in my hometown. Good to see dad and Catherine (my stepmother of 26 years). Mom was always my go-to for everything! But I love dad and I'm grateful to be with a parent. Even if to just be in his space and enjoy each other's company. Dad and I don't really talk about mom except for a few minutes here and there. Catherine and I talk about her more so: we had a nice conversation while dad was out in his shop one day. I share with her that mom had been my person for everything. The one I called when I had something to share, something going on, or needed to vent or seek advice. I think that's what I'll miss the most, it's hard not to have my beloved go-to.

Catherine shares that she'd felt that way about the relationship with her mom. She said she still misses her, and shares that she thinks the loss of a mother for a woman, is harder.... Her words fade out. She says she still says good morning and goodnight to her mother's picture on the wall next to her bed.

Dad had stepped outside and gone into the shop. When he came back in, he had an old picture of mom he'd found recently while cleaning up. It was a picture of her from before they were married. A sweet black and white picture of her standing (posing) in front of the fireplace in the house I grew up in. She was wearing a tight-fitting sweater and pencil pants from the early 70's. She was a beautiful woman. The picture was dirty so Catherine handed me Windex and a paper towel to clean it off. After cleaning it off and thanking him, I went upstairs and put it on my bedside table.

Chapter 28
A thing of the past

I feel there's definitely a part of me who wants to get away. I can see it in the spontaneously purchased ticket to Maryland. Yes, I had wanted to see dad and be with a parent and not be alone. But I'd also bought a ticket to Honolulu at the same time. Definite proof of wanting get out of dodge and away from my situation, or have somewhere to go and relax after wrapping up mom's affairs. Or did I just want to get away where I could lay in an unfamiliar space and just be with myself and my feelings? Be away from everything that was vying for my attention? Maybe both. Maybe all of it. It varies on the day and how I'm feeling, really.

I'd gone to Honolulu twice last year. Mom had mentioned to me that she'd like to go with me this year, and I'd inquired about ease of travel for the disabled both at the airport and the hotel. Now she'll be going with me in spirit.

When we die, especially suddenly, we most often leave behind the plans we'd made. I suppose unless we know it's on the way, right? And I'm sure we'd be sad about not being able to make plans for our future if death was imminent. She had future plans. She'd had a feeling she was running out of time, but death didn't seem imminent.

She had been thinking of Connie's trip, the doctors' visits when my sister returned the next week, an eye appointment she needed to make, and future visits from my younger sister and me. She was thinking about things she'd still like to do: Museums, whale watching, Hawaii. I bet she's seeing them now. No longer attached to earthly appointments and to do lists—just free to visit where she'd like.

In Maryland I'd seen an ad for a cute 2 story early 1900's house near the YMCA in Cambridge in the newspaper. On a whim I made an appointment to go see it. Could I live there again? I missed the heat, living in Seattle. It was more affordable than Vashon Island for sure and I always liked the water and the easy-going lifestyle. And there was a possibility to rent it out. Or Airbnb it while I wasn't in it. Or rent it out to dad and Catherine (although it had stairs, and they were trying to get away from those now).

After viewing it, I was tempted. So that night I wrote on a piece of paper, "Should I make an offer on the house?"

I read it a few times and stuck it on my bedside before closing my eyes and hoping for an answer.

That night I dreamt of the backyard of that house. There was a small shop in the backyard. In my dream there were people in the shop playing out some sort of drama. When they exited the shop, they tossed me a gun that hit the ground. I also heard the lyrics to the song *Jammin* by Bob Marley when I awoke.

The scene in the dream was a clear sign that if I purchased the house there'd be drama. And the song lyrics, "jammin' is a thing of the past," told me Cambridge was my past. I looked up jammin' and what it meant in Reggae, and it means dancing. Mom was a dancer and had owned and operated a dance studio in Cambridge until she and dad's divorce in 1995. Dancing was a thing of mom's past which I thought was very interesting. Yet another sign that it wasn't a good choice to put an offer on the house.

After getting back home from visiting my father in Maryland for an extended weekend, I crashed! I couldn't believe how weak and tired I felt. I questioned if I'd picked something up, or if I had the worst jet-lag ever. But no, sitting with it, I knew it was grief. I text a friend and she validates my feeling, "Sorry you're down, but that's part of the wave of grief. Love you. I'm here if you wanna jump on a call or stop by for a blessing or reading."

A few days later at my niece's bridal shower I shared this with my sister. She said how she was feeling the same way these last few days—and at the same time I was. It was nice to hear I wasn't alone, and It was like we were in synch with each other. We had even commented to each other how our clothing choice for the occasion matched, as well as our gift choice. We speculate that mom could've been influencing us from the other side and aiding us in our decisions for that day.

We felt she was around. On the drive to my sister's house I'd heard the song *abcdefu* come on the radio. I laughed that this was one of her songs mom communicated to me with. I snapped a quick little pic of the radio screen and sent it to Connie.

Chapter 29
The stages of grief

It's amazing how grief hits you in such diverse ways. I've experienced: physical aches and pains, joint pain and inflammation, weakness, both sleeplessness and sleeping longer, lethargy, mild headaches, low can't get out of my own way-- sadness, and extreme exhaustion. It's a can't get out of bed kind of tired that could keep me from doing the things I'd normally do.

I know from past experience that depression is a part of grief and can be the longest stage of grief. What's brought me out of my depression in the past is allowing myself to experience it, the loss, the sadness. I need to feel it, work with it, process it in various ways: Crying, writing, gratitude, volunteering, walking, nature, support of friends, affirmations, and emotional release exercises. I did anything and everything that came to me during my divorce, until one day when a sense of acceptance seemed to fall over me. A place where I accepted the loss, made some meaning out of it and was able to move on and start anew.

I wonder if it'll be the same with the loss of my mother. If one day, I'll wake up feeling like it's the first day of spring, or a weight has lifted, as I had felt a few months after my ex-husband moved out. It's not really like I'm starting "anew" in this situation. I'm not starting a new life all together like after a divorce. It's more like learning to live a new normal. Learning to live a life minus her full presence that has been a part of my life for so many years.

The hard part: The loss of her physical presence. I can't just pick up the phone to tell her something. That's what I miss the most. Before moving to Vashon, I'd lived in Poulsbo 13 years, and she'd lived down the road 15 minutes away. We'd spontaneously go for an errand or take the kids somewhere fun. But lately, 11 years later, me on Vashon, her in Suquamish, we only saw each other here and there. My older sister was more a part of her everyday life since my move. So, it's the phone time and the occasional visits I'll miss—the sharing of what's going on in my life and hers. She was my biggest fan. She and I had both missed the days when we'd just take off and do something fun. We had even spoke on it recently. Now I will miss our communication.

Immediately after her death, I think that sitting in the parking lot for what seemed like hours was the initial stage of grief: shock, which protects our minds from what we're not yet ready to deal with. Honestly, I still wonder if I'm still in a slight shock at times. Or fluctuating between shock, depression, and denial.

Denial for me feels like I'm just going about my days as usual. Like on the days that I hadn't spoken to mom. I'm just living the day and it's just a day that mom hasn't called, or I haven't wanted to call her. But there's no denial around her death. I know she's gone.

The bargaining stage I'm unsure about. I don't know if I've done this or that to avoid my pain. Is spirit communication a form of bargaining so that I can still have communication with her in this new way?

It is a family trait to busy ourselves when things are on our minds—like cleaning the whole kitchen or making ourselves busy around the house as to not have to think about it, or to process our thoughts in an active way. I usually do that when I'm upset about something or feeling angry. I've been the opposite with moms passing. Instead of being busy doing things, I don't have the energy to, and don't feel like it. I escape into binge-watching Netflix, or flying to see my father, or a solo trip to Honolulu. Maybe this is my coping mechanism at this moment? And I can see how people could easily choose unhealthy ways of coping in grief as a means of escape.

Anger: For me, anger has looked like questioning: "Could I have done something, noticed and shared something sooner in the car or at the hospital, not stressed her out by going from the car into her house before calling 911 to go back to the ER? I sometimes think, angrily, “Why did they discharge her the first time?” This has come up in conversation more than once, and I ask myself, why I hadn’t questioned more when I picked her up at the ER. They had me in and out so quickly. I wonder what I could have done if I’d had more time to access her.....

And another aspect of the anger; I can see how emotions could get high and a person could end up taking it out on a loved one. I often wonder if this is the stage that causes families to split during the post-death process. Anger is an easier emotion for many to deal with rather than their pain and sadness. People can harbor anger for years not knowing it’s really still covering up pain.

Depression: Where I was, after getting back from dad’s, and after the initial shock of mom’s passing. And I still dipped into depression here and there between good days or hours. There were feelings of being so tired and not wanting to do anything. There was no motivation. I’ve been trying to be easy with myself on this one. Usually, I’m posting for my business and things, and I have no motivation to do so. So I’m working on meeting myself where I’m at, and not expecting too much out of myself. I’m giving myself a pass.

And then there’s acceptance: I wonder if I’ve dipped my toe in here or if I’m treading water with denial. There’s a part of me that felt that mom’s passing was coming. I don’t want to say it’s made it easier, just that it wasn’t unexpected. I do think I was in denial or trying to be in denial during her death process. I was functioning as if she was going to pull through. I wanted her to. I told her to fight. I gave her reasons to stay: to see my younger sister Sara the next day or older sister Connie the following day. Maybe that was my bargaining. But at the same time, I knew death was a possibility, but didn't want to linger there as a possibility. I didn't want to believe it. So I pushed it aside, feeling that if I thought about it, it would manifest.

I think we all selfishly want our loved ones to stay with us a little bit longer—even if it's their time. Even if they're at peace with the process. Even if they know it's coming, like I think she did.

I wish she had been cognizant enough to discuss her feelings around her passing. On the ride home, she'd said she'd told the doctor she felt like she was going to die. How had she felt about that? Was she scared? At peace with it? Was there anything that she would've wanted to say or share?

If I had stopped to ask her how she felt about that statement, would she have been able to answer? I had asked, "Are you leaving us?" and she hadn't answered. I've wondered in the days following her death if she'd had any wishes or things she would've shared had I asked further. Before I called 911, she managed to get out, "Don't you dare!" She did not want me to call 911. What had that meant exactly? Was that her way of saying she wanted to die at home? Or did she just not want to go back to the hospital?

Of course, not wanting to think about the possibility of her death, and being in "save her, figure it out, she's not right, get her back to the ER' mode, I didn't even think to ask what her wishes were. Then again, she was barely able to communicate at that point, so I'm not even sure she would've been able to relay her feelings to me. I still wonder though.

Chapter 30
Unrealized anger

I'd been experiencing a little anxiety the last few nights and I wasn't quite sure why. Nothing was really coming to me except the possibility of a new symptom of grief. I'd been busy and not really paying attention to my process.

Last evening it hit me. I felt so much anger around my mother's death experience, my experience, and it hadn't "really" hit me yet. I found myself ruminating over the sequence of events, and strong emotions welled up, growing in feeling as the memories progressed. It was so strong, and I knew instantly this is what had been causing the anxiety— I needed to release the anger.

Years ago in school I learned a variety of emotional release exercises I use in my practice today. And when I feel that I have emotions to process, I walk myself through the same process.

I need to release this, so I communicate with my youngest son that I have the need to process some emotions, and I'd wanted to alert him so it didn't worry or scare him. This way he knows everything is okay while I safely process my anger.

It felt so good to release the anger! After I began the exercises: hand screams, pillow screams and punching, the emotion started to release. Before I knew it I was sobbing. I couldn't believe I'd been holding all those emotions inside without realizing it. No wonder I'd been experiencing anxiety.

After giving me some space to process, my youngest walks in and asks if he can join me. He snuggles in. I let him know I'm okay, that it was good to release the anger I'd been holding on to, good to cry and release the emotions; and thanked him for the space to do so. As we lie there, we share our feelings of loss and sadness around the loss of his grandmother.

A few minutes go by and out of his mouth he says, "blue dress." Astonished and shocked, I asked him, "What?" I can't believe he's saying "blue dress" as I flash back in my mind to the blue dress in the dream I'd had shortly after mom's passing.

He says, "I don't know, it just popped into my head and I thought I'd say it." I ask him, "Had I shared the dream about the dress?" I went on to explain the dream and I know it's a message from mom! She's there with us, there's no question. Where else would he get that thought?

I go on to share with him that it was his intuitive skills that were picking up on a message from his grandmother, and that he should pay attention to the things that pop into his mind because that's how they show up for me. He's delighted by this, and I think it's a great lesson in learning about his own gifts and how information shows up for him.

My tears drift away with the amazement. We share our joy with each other over the occurrence. We both say hello to mom, tell her that we love her, and say goodnight.

Chapter 31
I'm glad there was love

I had a conversation with an older woman on the ferry boat a few weeks ago on my way to the airport. I shared with her my loss, and she mirrored back the loss of her mother and grandmother she held dear to her heart.

People have always been inclined to share with me, so she also shared she'd come from a large family and had decided not to have children. She went on to say that she'd asked her belated husband on his deathbed if he'd regretted not having children. His answer was that there was a part of him that had. To this she'd replied, "Just imagine how'd they'd feel in this moment of loss if we had."

I respect her choice, and there are women who are called to mother in many other ways. And, her comment made me think: I feel the pain from heartbreak or loss of a loved one is in direct relationship to how much you allowed yourself to feel and love that person. Pain comes from the amount of attachment you allowed yourself to have. The heart feelings one feels in these times is a measurement of how much you allowed yourself to love another.

And I also imagine the feelings of guilt and regret are our measurements of how much we didn't allow ourselves to love.

I wouldn't give up the amount of pain I felt. I'd rather feel the pain of the loss of my loved ones than never to have spent the precious time with them, or the memories created with them, or the heart bond shared with them. I'm glad there was love.

Even in our challenged times I couldn't imagine a life without mom. How does that saying go? "It is better to have loved and lost than never to have loved at all".

Chapter 32
She's still near

I love how messages from the other side work. And when it happens, I know it's for me. I can just feel it inside, like a wink from the universe or a loved one. It's an inner knowing, a "yes, that's for me!"

A fun example of this was on a recent flight to see a girlfriend of mine.

There I was on the plane, waiting to take off. And usually, you get the airline attendants doing the normal pre-take off announcements. But not this time. Over the speakers I hear the captain announce that it's one of the attendant's birthday. Her name is Constance! Not every day you hear this type of thing on a plane. And it's not every day the woman whose birthday it happens to be is named Constance! I smile and give mom a little hello and an I love you. And I felt happy to know she's with me and watching over me during my travels.

I miss my mom terribly. I miss her just like she said I would. I miss her presence in my life. I miss being able to call her. I miss when she would call me. I feel an emptiness in my life that's almost indescribable except to say there's a hole in my life where she used to be.

But even with these feelings of sadness, grief, loss, and void, I know that she's with me. The signs were and are everywhere: The butterfly that almost hit me in the face in Hawaii. The white feathers that drifted in front of my path at the park on my way to dinner, and at the airport on my way home. The song that played over the radio on my way to my son's band concert. The 10:10 I've been seeing everywhere since her passing. The 4444 picture a friend sent the other night after I'd asked for a sign from the universe. The dancers from Shen Yun (a dance company based out of New York) that I'd had a conversation with while waiting for my table at Ramen Nakamura in Honolulu. Waking at 3:00 AM the night before last, briefly parting my eyelids to glimpse a white mist through my blurry eyes before drifting back to sleep.

I even woke up last night, the 2-month anniversary of her death, and reached for my phone beside the bed at the exact time of her death. In that moment something had told me to grab my phone. An idea had popped into my mind to roll over and look at my phone. If not for anything else, it reminded me that she's still around. That she's not really gone. She's gone in the physical sense, yes. But gone completely, no.

I've always believed our loved ones are never far from us. I believe they can communicate with us from the other side. But now I know it in a new way, because I experience it in a new way now that my mother has transitioned to the other side. She lets me know almost on a daily basis that she is still near. Still with me and supporting me from the other side.

Afterword

It's eight months after my mother's death, and this book is in the editing stage of publishing. My mother continues to communicate with me, letting me know she is with me and supporting me from the other side of the veil.

Whether it's a sound in the middle of the night that wakes me at 3:00 AM, or a flicker of the lightbulb, or air bubbles in the water jug in the night, or the printer cycling; I know they are little ways she lets me know she is around. Of course, she still shares song lyrics as I'm waking up. I am still greeted by butterflies, dragonflies, and hummingbirds, have had dream visitations, and find the occasional penny or dime.

On a recent visit to see my dad, my son Soren and I had an encounter with a butterfly. A large black butterfly with blue wing tips flew up in our faces and around us both for a solid minute before landing on a gutters edge above our heads. Soren has also gained closure around his last interaction with his grandmother. One day I happened upon a voicemail she'd left apologizing to Soren for her actions. This was very healing for him to hear it straight from her on the voicemail recording.

I feel death is also an opportunity for healing. Grief breaks us open and brings feelings, memories, family patterns, and intergenerational trauma to the surface where it may not have been available before. Perhaps the feelings and memories were suppressed or not allowed by the subconscious. As I've healed my grief, I've become aware of puzzle pieces that I hadn't put together yet, present themselves for healing. It's an opportunity for forgiveness of a loved one, or for ourselves if we choose, it's an opportunity for closure.

While in a meditative state at the end of a shamanic journey, I went into a waking dream. During this dream I saw my mother standing in clouds. Behind my mother appeared a tunnel of white light, and then beside her appeared Jesus with his palms facing forward. I felt a peace come over me in that moment, and knew she was at peace and in good hands.

A few days after that journey, I had the opportunity to release another layer of my grief and anger. I entered into an emotional release session, working with my grief and anger for about 20 minutes. Afterwards I went into a meditative state and had another vision of my mother. This time I saw a baby in utero. Then a little girl holding her father's hand while walking with him. In that moment I knew my mother had reincarnated like I'd suspected.

Our grief is a portal to spirit communication, it's an opening. I think when we receive afterlife communication there is a gift in it for people. Not only does it help reconcile grief, but there's the gift of knowing there is life after death, and that our consciousness goes on beyond our physical existence. My mother's presence has eased my grief and fears around my own life and death. Her communications has given people in her life a new perspective on the afterlife. They have given meaning to the loss and provided comfort in knowing our loved ones are okay.

So, I invite you to ask for a sign from your loved one. Say, "Give me a sign you are here with me." Then wait for it to happen. It may show up as a vision, a dream, a sound, a song, a smell, a penny, or something from nature, like a bird or butterfly or hummingbird. When you see, hear, or feel something, and then you think of them, know that they are communicating with you.

I remember when my second son was a toddler. My mother and I had gone to a nursery to purchase some flowers. On the drive I was sharing with my mother about angel communication. I told her all we had to do was ask for a sign and they would give us one. So, before we went inside the little garden shop, we asked for a sign. About fifteen minutes later a woman walked up to us and commented on my son's white blond hair: "Wow! Look at that angel hair!"

"Angel hair" was the sign we asked for. It's just that simple.

In loving memory

Constance Ann Eason

1936-2022

About the Author

A seer, seeker, and spiritual explorer, Liz Peterson is an intuitive energy healer, Reiki Master, spiritual coach, oracle reader, and podcaster. Liz has been a lifelong student of healing, personal growth, and metaphysics. She is the host of the podcast *Raise the Vibe with Liz,* dedicated to bringing today's psychics, healers, way-showers, inspirational speakers, and ascension leaders to an international audience. Her podcast mission is to heal the world, one guest at a time.

Mother of 4, Liz lives on a small island in the Pacific Northwest, where she enjoys all life has to offer. She uses her natural born abilities, and her personal journey of healing, transformation, and empowerment in her work with individuals. With love and compassion, it's her personal mission to assist others on their spiritual journey of awakening and healing. Liz empowers and guides people to clear and release stuck energy, blocks, trauma while activating the body's natural healing process. You can find her offerings on -

www.lizshealingtouch.com

.

Made in the USA
Columbia, SC
08 March 2023